Wisdom of the Ages

Wisdom of the Ages
The Mystique of the African American Preacher

Edited by Robert Johnson-Smith II

Judson Press ® Valley Forge

Wisdom of the Ages: The Mystique of the African American Preacher
© 1995 Robert Johnson-Smith II

Bible quotations in this volume are from the HOLY BIBLE: *New International Version*, copyrighted © 1973, 1978, 1984. Used by permission of Zondervan Bible Publishers.

Library of Congress Cataloging-in-Publication Data
Wisdom of the ages : the mystique of the African American preacher / Robert Johnson-Smith II, editor.
    p. cm.
    Includes bibliographical references (p.).
    ISBN 0-8170-1225-7 (pbk. : alk. paper)
    1. Afro-Americans—Religion. 2. Afro-American clergy.
3. Pastoral theology. I. Johnson-Smith, Robert.
BR563.N4W555 1995
277.3'082'08996073—dc20   95-22941

Printed in the U.S.A.

95 96 97 98 99 00 01 02   8 7 6 5 4 3 2 1

To my wife
Janine
I love you.
Thank you for believing in me and in this project.

This book is dedicated in memory of
my great grandfather
Rev. "Doc" Smith
Where the legacy began

my grandfather
Rev. Dr. J. H. L. Smith
Former Pastor of Ebenezer Baptist Church; Chicago, Illinois

my brother
Rev. Everett Newton Smith
Former Pastor of Taylor Memorial Baptist Church; Philadelphia, Pennsylvania

my mother
Jennie Mae Smith
Who taught me to take all sermons to the cross

in honor of
my father
Rev. Dr. Robert Johnson-Smith
Pastor of Salem Baptist Church of Jenkintown; Jenkintown, Pennsylvania

and in anticipation of
my sons
Robert Johnson-Smith III
and
Cameron Laurence Smith
. . . may the legacy live on.

Contents

Acknowledgments

I must begin by thanking God for giving me the vision for this work and the strength to see it through. Because of the cooperation I received from all who contributed to this book, I know that God was in the midst.

I would also like to express my sincere gratitude to all of the contributors in this book, especially those who had absolutely no idea of who I was but took the time to share their wisdom with me. Thank you for your vision in seeing the need for a work of this type. I would also like to thank all of the secretaries and administrative assistants of the contributors, who assisted in securing the interviews for this book. Your kindness and patience is greatly appreciated.

Special thanks to my publisher, Harold W. Rast; associate publisher, Kristy Arnesen Pullen; former marketing manager, William J. Key; editorial manager, Mary M. Nicol; editorial assistant, Victoria W. McGoey; copyeditor, Kathleen Hayes; and the entire staff at Judson Press. Thank you for having faith in me, an unknown writer, and for having faith in this project.

I must also thank my Salem Baptist Church family. God has truly blessed me with a loving congregation. Thank you for your continued support. Special thanks to Deacon Venord Cowan for driving me to a revival at the Triumph Baptist Church in Philadelphia, where I received the first interviews for this book.

I am indebted to my history professor at Morehouse College, Dr.

Leroy Davis, who sparked in me a new way of thinking that changed my life forever. I thank him for teaching me about the politics of language and that all language has political connotations. Also, special thanks to my advisor at Lutheran Theological Seminary, Katie Day, for assisting me with the bibliography for this book.

I am also indebted to Dr. Frank B. Mitchell, Jr., and Dr. William H. Gray III, who opened their pulpits to me as a seminary student.

Fraternal thanks to the men of the Omega Psi Phi Fraternity, Inc.

Finally, I must thank my family. To my sister, Renee, thank you for your never-ending encouragement. To my father, Robert Johnson-Smith Sr., thank you for your support throughout my entire life and for the wisdom that you have shared with me. Thank you to my wife, Janine, without whom this book would have never been completed. Thank you for all of your help. To my boys, Robert III and Cameron, you make it all worthwhile. I also thank the members of my extended family for their support.

Introduction

Every preacher must have a gallery and a garden. One should have a gallery where you reach up and commune with the wisdom of the ages—a gallery where you can talk with Jeremiah or Socrates or Shakespeare or Langston Hughes. One must also have a garden where you can pull up plants out of your own experience and be able to say, like Paul, "I know in whom I believe."

—*The late Sandy Ray to Otis Moss, Jr.*

My mother always told me that you can find something good in every situation. It must be true because it appeared that nothing good was coming from the treacherous snowstorms that hit eastern Pennsylvania during the winter of 1993–1994. Something good did happen. While sitting at home wondering how my car was going to get shoveled out and looking at a copy of Dorothy Wimbush Riley's book, *My Soul Looks Back: 'Less I Forget*, the idea for this book emerged. It was an idea born in the midst of a storm . . . but its time had come.

Being a fourth-generation preacher, the concept of wisdom being passed down through the ages has always fascinated me. As a boy my eyes would see the great ones as they graced the pulpit of the Salem Baptist Church of Jenkintown, Pennsylvania. They all came through, from Benjamin E. Mays to Gardner C. Taylor to Martin Luther King, Jr., to Jesse L. Jackson. My summer vacations were filled with barbecues populated by clergy from all over the nation, including a young pastor named William H. Gray III, under whom

I would later serve at the Bright Hope Baptist Church in Philadelphia. As I watched the great preachers and pastors of my tradition, I always used to ask the question, What is it that makes these preachers tick? Where did they get the wisdom and savvy that allowed them to take virtually nothing and create ministries and legacies that would thrive for generations? I could not give the seminaries the credit for this type of wisdom; some of the great ones had not set foot in the seminaries. This is not to take anything away from the seminaries, for the seminaries have their place. But much of the wisdom that these preachers possessed and still possess was not learned within the walls of higher learning. This wisdom came from experience and from an informal transmittal process called "sitting at the feet of," in which a young preacher would "sit at the feet of" an experienced preacher and listen to stories and anecdotes about ministry and receive tried and tested practical advice about pastoring African American people.

Recently, society has popularized the word *mentoring*. For the African American preacher throughout history, mentoring has been a common practice. It was not done for practical reasons exclusively; it was also a matter of survival. For the most part, many of the other types of support mechanisms that were afforded clergy of other ethnic groups did not exist for the African American preacher. Wisdom was passed from one generation of preacher to the next through a tradition that came with us from the homeland—the oral tradition. While seminaries, forums, conferences, and other arenas have afforded the African American preacher the opportunity to share and dialogue about this wisdom, the transmittal process is still basically the same. This book is an attempt to put some of this wisdom on paper.

Wisdom is an abstract word. Its meaning varies from person to person. It has been described as "knowledge," "insight," "sound judgement," and "common sense." Wisdom is best described as a combination of all of these terms and perhaps others, all yielding some type of positive, useful, practical information.

Wisdom is something that is sought after by people of all races, ages, genders, and socio-economic levels. What is more interesting than this is that it can be obtained by all people, regardless of who they are, if they are willing to seek it *and* receive it. Wisdom is an equal opportunity concept.

From the Hebrew word *hokmah, wisdom* is used in Scripture to describe a sense of knowledge of the principles of right living gained through observation, experience, and reflection. The book of Proverbs probably gives us the best description of wisdom. Proverbs 1:7 states, "The fear of the LORD is the beginning of knowledge, but fools despise wisdom and discipline." Proverbs 4:5-8 states: "Get wisdom, get understanding; do not forget my words or swerve from them. Do not forsake wisdom, and she will protect you; love her, and she will watch over you. Wisdom is supreme; therefore get wisdom. Though it costs all you have, get understanding. Esteem her, and she will exalt you; embrace her, and she will honor you." True wisdom can be helpful in any arena of life. For the preacher or pastor, the attainment of it is truly an asset. It is my hope that this book will help clergy in their quest for wisdom.

When I began this project, my initial fear was that the egos of some preachers, pastors, and scholars would prevent this work from becoming a reality. I discovered that, for the most part, this was not the case. Because of the cooperation of the clergy, I was able to secure interviews with over one hundred pastors, preachers, and scholars representing eighteen denominational groups. Fifteen of those I interviewed were women. With the exception of a few, all of the clergypersons I contacted responded and granted me an interview for this book.

The list of contributors that I compiled for this work began with the November 1993 *Ebony* magazine article entitled "The Fifteen Greatest Preachers"; many of the contributors from the *Ebony* study are included in this book. Some of the contributors are among our nation's greatest living theologians, writers, and administrators. I've also included a number of outstanding preachers and pastors who have had exemplary ministries but have not gotten the national recognition that others have received. Finally, the book contains entries from some relatively obscure clergypersons who are struggling to pastor the congregations with which God has blessed them. What is important here is that any preacher, pastor, scholar, or theologian who has truly tried to answer the call of God and has labored in the vineyard has attained some degree of wisdom that needs to be shared with others.

Most of the interviews were obtained over the telephone. However, a number of face-to-face interviews were conducted in Philadelphia, Boston, and Los Angeles. Only a few interviews were received through written responses.

Chapter 1 is a scholarly chapter that sets the stage for the rest of the book. It discusses the impact that the oral tradition has made in the African American church and in the lives of African American preachers. The remainder of the book consists of quotations from the contributors to this book in response to questions that were asked of them in the interviews. In chapter 2, participants were asked to share their wisdom regarding sermon preparation. Chapter 3 discusses wisdom as it relates to pastoral care, and chapter 4 focuses on wisdom regarding church administration. In chapter 5, each contributor was asked to share some wisdom with young pastors beginning their first pastorate; the advice is in fact beneficial to any pastor entering a new pastorate, regardless of age. The last chapter focuses on wisdom recalled from memories after having been passed on to today's clergy from those who have already made their transition from this life to the next.

As one reads these quotations, it my hope that they will be digested slowly. While some may be brief in length, they are extremely profound. Read the quotes over and over and, if need be, contact the contributor personally to gain a greater understanding of the words he or she has shared.

I must make a few disclaimers in regard to this book. First, while it is called *The Wisdom of the Ages: The Mystique of the African American Preacher*, this work focuses on preachers who are of the Christian faith. It is not my intention to discredit preachers of other faiths within the African American community. Their voices are also important, but they are not the focus of this particular work. In regard to inclusive language, I have attempted to be inclusive throughout this book. Of course, with the quotations of the contributors, I used the language that was shared with me in each interview. Some contributors were very conscious of inclusive language; others were not. If there is a question about a particular contributor, the reader should contact the contributor directly for further clarification. Finally, while this book does expand upon the listings in the *Ebony* article, it should be noted that countless other clergypersons could have been included in this work. It was not my intention to omit anyone but to obtain a representative sample of African American preachers. To me, anyone who dares to proclaim the gospel of Jesus Christ is great. Perhaps this work will prompt other volumes of this type to be written in the future.

It is my hope that preachers of today will be able to use the wisdom of the ages to help build the kingdom of God here on earth and that they will pass it on to those who are yet to come. May God bless those who have been, those who are, and those who will be.

Chapter 1

Talkin' Loud, Sayin' Something
The Oral Tradition and the African American Preacher

In 1972 James Brown, the "Godfather of Soul," recorded a song entitled "Talkin' Loud and Sayin' Nothing," in which he describes people who talk a lot but have nothing to say. This has *not* been the case with the African American preacher. From the first time a slave "told the story" in the tobacco fields of Mississippi; to the oratory of a Martin Luther King, Jr., on the steps of the Lincoln Memorial; to the eloquence of a Jesse L. Jackson at the Democratic Convention, the African American preacher has always had a message to give to the world. It is a message born out of severe oppression and a quest for survival. The African American preacher took what he or she could from the sometimes-twisted theology of the slave master, the remnants of culture and religion from Africa, and the work of the Holy Spirit, and combined them into what has developed into African American religious thought. Today, the African American church is the end result of over two hundred years of divine inspiration, trial and error, wit, formal education, prayer, black and white theologies—plus blood, sweat, and tears. The wisdom that has been derived from this ecclesiastical mix has been passed down from one preaching generation to the next. Transmitted orally, this wisdom has been used by African American pastors and preachers to lead the churches of the past and the present. While technologies may change, this wisdom will probably help to lead the churches of the future.

It started in African tradition. Nya Kwiawon Taryor, Sr., describes this tradition as "all the oral information that has been handed down from past generations of Africans to their offspring about certain beliefs, customs, religious practices, thought patterns, mannerisms, ethical systems, socio-political systems, forms of education, etc."[1]

Much of this concept of oral teaching was called "storytelling." People in their respective villages could learn the lessons of life from hearing stories told by the elders. This was the basis for survival and cohesion in the family tribal unit. It was the way social institutions were maintained. Storytelling was used to entertain, to settle disputes, and was sometimes combined with music, dance, and poetry. There were no books, no writings, no classrooms—just traditions kept alive by an active memory. While some may consider it primitive, this method was and continues to be an effective, legitimate system of learning and teaching. Through the oral tradition, boys and girls learned about their ancestors, their roles in life, the life in the village, and the afterlife.[2] It was not uncommon for young people to attend the meetings of their elders. The young people would watch the elders in action as they made important decisions and handled disputes. It was also at these meetings that the young people would hear the elders talk about their history and the laws and customs of their own society.[3]

This method of teaching would travel with those who were brought to these shores and forced into slavery. While many white Christians used religion and the Bible as a means to further oppress and subjugate those who were enslaved, some Christian abolitionists put their lives on the line in order to teach those who were enslaved. In 1853 Margaret Douglass, a Christian abolitionist, was imprisoned in Norfolk, Virginia, for teaching prayer and reading of the Bible to slaves. The law that prosecuted Douglass was passed in 1831, shortly after the Nat Turner insurrection. Eventually all slave states, with the exception of Tennessee, restricted instruction of slaves to oral means. By 1855, in nine of fifteen slave states, it was illegal to distribute Bibles to slaves.[4] Because the slaves were not allowed to be formally educated, the oral method of teaching and learning provided important education for the slaves. This method of transmission was used by the slaves to learn what they needed to know in order to survive, including the Bible.[5]

In a discussion about Christian abolitionist Rev. Charles C. Jones and the effect of oral instruction, Milton Sernet writes:

> Although Northern critics were certain that religious training without letters would fail, the Southern missionaries quickly resigned themselves to conformity to the slave code. Jones felt that instruction by oral means would work because of the remarkable memory of the slave children he catechized. "Their memory," he wrote, "is their book." Once the Biblical story had been told to them, it was "stamped on the tablet of memory forever."[6]

This tradition would continue even after the slaves were freed, yet it would take on a different twist. Ella Mitchell states that

> oral tradition performed the same function after the slaves were freed, with only two changes: the restrictions on movement were reduced, diminishing somewhat the level of enforced intimacy in the extended family; and there was a massive new emphasis on formal education, reading, writing and arithmetic. However, the latter did not take the place of oral tradition in the deeper matters of how to cope in oppression and the development of an adequate belief system. In fact, formal education itself was often fused or blended with oral tradition forms of instruction in many creative ways.[7]

While this was true, it must be noted that the early African American preachers, the "Black Fathers," did not have the doors of the established religious schools swing open to them. During the latter part of the 1800s, some African American preachers were able to get a formal education. Most learned whatever they could from wherever they could and used this knowledge to build and pastor the early African American churches.[8]

In his writings, Henry Mitchell discusses many early African American preachers who used a wholistic method of education that, for the most part, relied on the oral tradition and any other information that could be obtained:

> I think of my own home church pastor (obviously before my

time), a man by the name of Poindexter, about whom Carter G. Woodson, the black historian, wrote a great deal. Poindexter got his education as a barber, across the street from the statehouse at Columbus, Ohio. He was pastor of the Second Baptist Church for some forty years. He held high political (elected) office. He was obviously a very intelligent first-rate leader. But the education that he received was while people thought he was cutting their hair, but he was actually "picking their brains."[9]

Of Dr. Jacob Benjamin Boddie, from Nashville, North Carolina, who had only a sixth-grade education, Mitchell writes:

> From a formal point of view, Boddie had no college or seminary training whatsoever, and his only degrees were honorary doctors. Yet he . . . read constantly and soaked up information from everywhere. . . . The properly chastened concern for education learning that characterized men like Dr. Boddie . . . might be styled as seeking helpful truth wherever it might be found, while maintaining a basic commitment to black religion in confident communication with Black people.[10]

Charles Hamilton, in his classic book, *The Black Preacher in America*, talks about Father Lorenthro Wooden, who was a Morehouse student when Martin Luther King, Jr., was a student. After graduating from Morehouse, Wooden would go on to three theological seminaries, never graduating from any of them. He also struggled with the principles of the African Methodist Episcopal church. After years of searching, he went to Miami, Florida, and worked with an Episcopal priest who was from the Bahamas. Wooden learned the value of the oral teaching when this Episcopal priest shared with him this advice during a conversation: "If you are going to pastor black people, you damn well better throw away the books you learned from in seminary and look at the people you are dealing with."[11]

As time went on, it is true that more African American preachers gained the opportunity to get formal training in the religious schools of the United States and abroad. Today, many doors are open for African American seminary students. It should be noted, however, that while the seminaries may share some useful information that the African American preacher can use, they do not impart the wisdom and practical skills that he or she will need to pastor African American people. While there have been some resources printed in recent years that describe some of the practices and methods of African American preachers, most of this information is obtained orally, just as it had been transmitted in early African tradition. This is not to say that African American preachers should abandon the Eurocentric seminaries. Graduation from these institutions does provide a certain amount of prestige and legitimacy in certain religious circles. But the African American preachers should hold on to this tradition of oral transmission and recognize it, without apology, as a very pertinent part of their education. It will be this aspect of their education that will make them or break them in the African American church. While the seminaries will teach us about the great European theologians and Eurocentric methods of pastoring, and the African American preacher is wise to learn this information, he or she must also know how to "deal with the folks." This knowledge comes from "sitting at the feet of" experienced, seasoned preachers. It comes from talking with those who have weathered the storm in their ministries and hearing how they made it, what they had to deal with, how they handled situations, and how the Lord has brought them through. This knowledge also comes from hearing the stories of the older preachers as they talk about the experiences in the world of the African American church. These experiences, legends, and myths are a part of the African American religious culture, and just as the experiences, legends, and myths in ancient Africa were used to educate one generation to the next, the same is true today. It is ironic that the Eurocentric method of education is done in a written fashion, that is, through reading books and writing information. But, in most disciplines on the doctorate level, both written and oral exams are required for graduation. If we check the record, we will also notice that the early church was founded, developed, and grown through people *"telling* the story" to others.

Notes

1. Nya Kwiawon Taryor, Sr., *Impact of the African Tradition on African Christianity* (Chicago: Strugglers' Community Press, 1984), 262.

2. Ella P. Mitchell, "Black Nurture," in *Black Church Life-Styles*, comp. Emmanuel L. McCall (Nashville: Broadman Press, 1986), 49-50.

3. Taryor, 91.

4. Milton C. Sernet, *Black Religion and American Evangelism* (Metuchen, N.J.: The Scarecrow Press, Inc., 1975), 65-66.

5. Ella P. Mitchell in McCall, 50-51.

6. Sernet, 66.

7. Ella P. Mitchell in McCall, 58-59.

8. Henry H. Mitchell, "Black Preaching," in McCall, 116.

9. Ibid., 116.

10. Henry H. Mitchell, *Black Preaching* (New York: Harper and Row, 1979), 61-63.

11. Charles V. Hamilton, *The Black Preacher in America* (New York: William Morrow & Co., 1972), 1951-97.

Chapter 2

Saturday Night Blues
Wisdom on Preparing a Sermon

The preacher must choose a biblical text and focus on the needs of the congregation.

—*Olin P. Moyd*

Seek the needs of the people whom you are addressing. Many times, during the sermon, the preacher answers questions that nobody is asking.

—*Wallace S. Hartsfield*

A text out of context is a pretext.

—*Jesse L. Jackson*

The preacher must first know the pain, the hurt, the suffering, the emptiness, the voids of the experiences of the people. Then, the preacher can develop a sermon that speaks to them and gives them hope.

—*Cecil Williams*

Read a lot.

—*Renita J. Weems*

Only God can finish a sermon. Preaching is a partnership between the preacher and the Holy Spirit.

—*Zan Holmes*

Before the preacher can make the text contemporary or practical, the preacher must be able to transpose himself or herself across the generations, across the centuries, and actually sit down in the midst of the text. One must capture the sights and sounds of the text. One must get into the very life of the text. I preach as a participant of the text rather than a spectator of the text.

—Charles E. Booth

Take the time.

—Calvin O. Butts III

The preacher must pray for the cultivation of the eye and the ear. The pastor must have sensitivity and perception to see and hear the sermons that are all around us and be open to see and hear the bombardment of sermons that are begging to be preached through our lives, our ministries, and the world. This allows our preaching to be scripturally based and life-experience based. What this generation needs is preaching that intersects reality.

—Fred A. Lucas, Jr.

Preachers must first pray and ask God to open their eyes and their heart.

—Susan D. Newman

In preparing the sermon, always read the Scriptures out loud. They were originally oral before they were written. When you hear them out loud, they will change in you and in your hearing of them.

—Anthony Campbell

For every minute we speak, it takes one hour of preparation.

—Katie G. Cannon

The text of the message ought to be supported by the best that one can gather by using all of his or her academic powers and intellect, while at the same time never hesitating to allow one's imagination, faith, and hope to take wings.

—*Otis Moss, Jr.*

The preparation of the sermon is determined in large part by the preacher's objective and the treatment of the passage of Scripture. The treatment of the passage of Scripture involves knowing who said it, why it was said, under what circumstances was it said, and the conditions of the times in which the utterance was made.

—*Caesar A. W. Clark*

The pastor must be familiar with the original language of the text.

—*Mack King Carter*

Read widely and remember that the development of the sermon is a process and not an event.

—*John H. Adams*

Don't think more highly of yourself than you are. Remember that you are a vessel.

—*Beverly J. Shamana*

For weekly preaching, start Monday morning. Select the Scripture, do your reading, get your background information, do your formalizing. Keep in mind preaching with the Bible in one hand and the newspaper in the other.

—*Cecil Murray*

Be sure that your spiritual foundation is in good order.

—*Corneilius Henderson*

Try to write down in one sentence the word that God has given you for the people for that occasion. This should be extracted from the biblical text and applied to a live, current situation. This

will save the sermon from rambling and losing focus. This is the
proposition.
　　　　　　　　　　　　　　　　　　　—*Samuel D. Proctor*

Be sure to spiritually prepare yourself. The sermon will be
the natural result.
　　　　　　　　　　　　　　　　　　　—*Frederick K. C. Price*

Prepare and preach to yourself and hopefully you will reach
such a depth that there will be a vein of commonality with all the
people.
　　　　　　　　　　　　　　　　　　　—*Arlee Griffin, Jr.*

Preach on something that is exciting to you, something you
have seen with fresh eyes.
　　　　　　　　　　　　　　　　　　　—*Delores Carpenter*

Pray and be sure that it [the sermon] is based on sound biblical
principles. Stand up on Sunday morning and deliver it as best you
can.
　　　　　　　　　　　　　　　　　　　—*Leon H. Sullivan*

The sermon should be prepared prayerfully and carefully.
Make sure that the message is a message that the Lord will have
you preach. The preacher must go into prayer and open his head
and heart to the Holy Spirit. Then God will indeed direct that
preacher in terms of the message that he would have him to share
with the people of God.
　　　　　　　　　　　　　　　　　　　—*Michael N. Harris*

Start with the text. Let the text speak. I would rather have a
text that produces a sermon than a sermon looking for a text.
　　　　　　　　　　　　　　　　　　　—*T. Garrott Benjamin, Jr.*

The sermon must have a focus. The preacher must be able to

answer the question, "What am I saying?" This should be done in one or two sentences.

—J. Wendell Mapson, Jr.

The preacher must strive to make the sermon biblically based and theologically sound. It should address some human, contemporary need. It should be understandable and draw people to Christ. There should be some challenge to commitment.

—Joseph E. Lowery

Preach from the great themes of the Bible.

—James H. Evans, Jr.

Be prayerful, biblical, personal, relevant, helpful, and grounded in the Spirit. Be strong in your delivery, first to yourself and to those who hear you. Never quit!

—J. Jerome Cooper

Allow time for the preparation of the sermon. Leave Saturdays as free as possible for meditation.

—Suzan Johnson Cook

The sermon should be steeped in much prayer. It should be the voice of God speaking to the needs of the people. We do not have to lambaste people all the time. We must remember that the gospel is the Good News.

—William B. Moore

One has to be gotten hold of by a situation or by a Scripture or by both. This is crucial to preparation, because once that happens, there is a certain excitement about proceeding with it.

—Gardner C. Taylor

Go into preparation of the sermon prayerfully, inviting the visitation of the Holy Spirit.

—Repsie Warren

Preaching ought to be about a problem to solve in a person's life. The preacher must be aware of the itch that he or she is trying to scratch and the hurt that he or she is trying to heal.

—*Aidsand Wright-Riggins*

Listen to yourself, listen to the Word, and listen to the people.

—*Gus Roman*

I approach preaching as a theologian. I start out with an idea of what I want to say. Then I go to the Bible and do a thorough research job on the text and its content. The sermon must be Bible based and be based on good exegesis.

—*J. Deotis Roberts*

The preacher must sit where the people sit. The preacher must go to the parish before going to the study.

—*J. Alfred Smith, Sr.*

The preacher must find a way to live in the text to be able to thoroughly understand emotionally as well as intellectually the circumstances and the context in which the people lived then. If you can live in the text, then you have an opportunity to interpret what the text meant to those to whom it was originally given. Then you can make the transference from its "was-ness" to its "is-ness," that is, from what it meant in the ancient world to what it means for us in modern times.

—*H. Beecher Hicks, Jr.*

Make sure that you are listening to hear what the Word of God is saying today.

—*Jeremiah A. Wright, Jr.*

Saturate the process with prayer, realizing that we are never in charge of the process. The preacher must approach the process with a certain amount of vulnerability. This allows the sermon to live in the preacher before it is ever preached in the pulpit. We must remember that all our efforts, skills, and research are placed in God's hands for service.

—*Prathia Hall Wynn*

You must smell it, taste it, feel it, and experience it yourself; then you can share it with the people.

—*Ella P. Mitchell*

Let the text do the talking.

—*William A. Jones, Jr.*

The preacher must take a look at the issues that are relative to the people in which he serves and speak to them. The Bible should be the primary source.

—*Joe S. Ratliff*

Have a long period of prayer. Read thoroughly the Scriptures, several versions. Consult solid commentaries. Then add appropriate illustrations so that people will be able to grasp and take something with them.

—*Thomas Kilgore, Jr.*

Pray so that the message that comes through you is not your message but God's message.

—*Joy Clark*

Honor the sermon opportunity as an occasion for serious preparation. When doing regular preaching, that is, Sunday to Sunday, the sermon topic should be selected by Thursday of the week.

—*Cain Hope Felder*

Sermons are everywhere. The preacher must be open to all that life has to offer. Listen to people, observe people, listen to what is being said on television, read all the time, and sermons will come to you. Study the Bible, more than just the King James Version. Follow the Christian calendar. Preach in series.

—*Samuel B. McKinney*

Prepare prayerfully. Prayer should be the foundation of the sermon idea process.   —*Frank M. Reid III*

Make sure that you have read the guide book, the Bible.

—*E. Edward Jones*

Start in the depths of your own soul with a real conviction of what you are going to preach about.   —*Henry H. Mitchell*

The sermon must fit the people or congregation that is being preached to. The preacher should pray over the subject and then take the subject and fit it to a passage of Scripture in the Bible. The next step is to make it practical, that is, how this sermon can be applied to the lives of the people. The preacher should preach to the people about something that is relevant to them.

—*T. J. Jemison, Sr.*

Have a clear and concrete objective. The sermon ought to raise the question, "What am I aiming at?" It should have some form of an outline so that you systematize what you are saying, so that it will be digestible. It should be both true and divinely approved.   —*Manuel L. Scott, Sr.*

Read until you get full, pray until you get hot, then let go.

—*Alvin O. Jackson*

Prepare your sermon with the understanding that the sermon is for you, as well as for the people that you are preaching to.

—Sherman G. Hicks

The preacher must get into the text and understand it. If it becomes clear to you and you have determined the behavioral purpose that you want your hearers to experience or identify with, then you can go on with preparation.

—Ella P. Mitchell

Make sure that you saturate yourself in the lives of the congregation and the setting in which those lives are lived.

—William J. Shaw

Start preparing early.

—Bennett W. Smith

Sit with the people and understand what their hurts and hopes are. Preaching is not done in isolation.

—Amos Brown

Sermon preparation must begin with prayer. Then, the preacher must search the Scriptures under the direction of the Holy Spirit to find an appropriate passage. The preacher must then study the passage to determine how it relates to everyday life.

—Benjamin Smith

Let your preparational priority be preaching the Bible, not quoting from scholars. The most profound sermon is usually one that is simplest and easiest to understand.

—M. Marquette Peace, Jr.

Be imaginative. Let your imagination be fluid and flowing so that the text becomes alive. —*William E. Hayman, Jr.*

The preacher must consult God first. Listen for his instruction. The sermon comes from God as his message for his children. The preacher must get out of the way, so that God can express himself in his own way through the preacher.

—*Johnnie Colemon*

The sermon should expose a truth that will be valuable to the preacher and to those who will discover it.

—*Frank B. Mitchell, Jr.*

The sermon should grow out of the pastor's discernment of the needs of the people that he or she is serving. It should also grow out of the circumstances of the country and the events in history that are taking place at the particular time.

—*James C. Perkins*

Focus the sermon so that it meets at least the minimal requirements of a good essay. Be clear, comprehensive, and concise.

—*David T. Shannon, Sr.*

The preacher must know his subject matter. He must keep in mind the congregation that he will be delivering the sermon to. The hearers of sermons are real, and the pastor should know what types of experiences the congregation is going through. Know your subject and know your people. —*Robert Johnson-Smith, Sr.*

Give yourself enough time to prepare so that you can do a

thorough job in terms of proper interpretation of the text, as well as in terms of allowing the text to minister to your spirit.

—*William D. Watley*

Preachers should have a daily devotion time.

—*Susan D. Newman*

Every sermon ought to be prepared in an atmosphere of prayer with a message, idea, or Scripture that has captured one's inner being to the extent that you are convinced that it is worth sharing with the congregation.

—*Otis Moss, Jr.*

Start early in your preparation so that you can live with your sermon text. Then appropriate illustrations and stories will have sufficient time to help mold and make the sermon into what God will have it to be.

—*Ralph E. Blanks*

Always know how you want to end the sermon. The celebration of the sermon has to be clear and clearly planned. Unless you can celebrate the message, it will not be a memorable message.

—*Aidsand Wright-Riggins*

First you should find a text that grabs you. From this text, you should develop a title. After you have decided on your thesis, that is, the idea that you want to get across, you should then write it in a couple of sentences. Then, without looking in any books, empty your mind of everything you can think of on that topic. You should write until you feel that there is nothing else in you. Then, you can consult commentaries or other volumes. This will assure your creativity.

—*Lawrence E. Carter, Sr.*

Make sure to take the necessary time for preparation.
—*Dennis W. Wiley*

Be true to the biblical text.
—*William H. Gray III*

The preacher must feel the text to identify with it as dialogue between the text and the person.
—*Forrest Harris*

Study diligently. Write for the ear.
—*Wallace C. Smith*

Follow the guidance of the Holy Spirit.
—*Sara Potter Smith*

Make the sermon relevant to everyday life.
—*Jesse Brown, Jr.*

Choose a day of the week to begin your sermon preparation and don't let anything deviate you from it.
—*Mack H. Smith*

The pastoral sermon is just one part of the overall mandate of caregiving. The pastor must avoid loading up on Sunday morning with everything we want to see happen in the lives of the people who are gathered during worship. The pastor must remember that there are other avenues to minister to people, such as counseling, programs, visitation, and administration. The question the preacher must ask is, "Where does this particular message fit in the overall scheme of what God is trying to do in this particular place?"
—*H. Dean Trulear*

The pastor must first select the subject. This subject should be pondered for a while to see if there is a connection between it and the people to whom it will be spoken. Then the preacher should write all he or she can about the particular subject. Then a passage of Scripture should be found that suits that theme so that the message will come out of a scriptural background.

—*J. Wendell Mapson, Sr.*

If you preach to your own heart hunger, you will reach the people. If you preach to your own fears, weaknesses, and needs, you will identify with the people.

—*J. Alfred Smith, Sr.*

The sermon should be biblically based and relevant with respect to the times in which we live, so that God's Word has a meaning for today. In the words of Caesar Clark, "The sermon should be intellectually responsible."

—*Michael N. Harris*

Never give quick fixes to what people are going through.

—*Cecil Williams*

Let the words of the text leap off of the page to you.

—*Susan D. Newman*

Write a sermon every week, whether you use it or not.

—*Anthony Campbell*

The message ought to be biblically based, so at least, if the message itself turns out not to be worth hearing, the people can at least leave with a worthwhile Scripture.

—*Otis Moss, Jr.*

The sermon must be approached with prayer. There must be an openness to receive illumination from the Word of God.

—*G. Daniel Jones*

The preacher must protect one's preparation time. The parish

will not give you the time, the community will not give you the time, but the pastoral preacher must have the ability to say no and make preaching the priority. The people may be upset, but they will forgive you for not being at the PTA meeting, or for not giving the prayer at the NAACP banquet on Saturday night, but they will not forgive you for striking out in the pulpit on Sunday morning.
                                                            —*J. Alfred Smith, Sr.*

There are three things that are necessary in preparing a sermon. The first is the use of a text. A text is used to grant the hearers and the preacher a common foundation. It is also used to provide a common focus and gain a common faith. The second thing that is necessary is to understand the need of the audience. A sermon that is preached without some sense of need is a sermon that is not properly aimed or directed. Where there is a sufficient understanding of the needs of the audience, then the text can be chosen with wisdom, and its meaning can be focused with precision. The third thing necessary in preaching is to understand the situation or the setting in which the sermon will be delivered. This will grant the preacher a sense of timing, a sense of urgency, and will allow a sense of immediacy to influence how the sermon is treated because of the setting in which it is delivered.
                                                            —*James E. Massey*

Go to the preparation of the sermon with the events that affect people's lives in mind.
                                                            —*Jacquelyn Grant*

In preparing the sermon, there needs to be prayerful, quiet time.
                                                            —*Albert Campbell*

The preacher must seek to lift the hearts and spirits of people in their preaching.
                                                            —*Floyd Massey, Jr.*

God has a word for God's people in every situation. The word that God has for that particular people has to be pursued in the supernatural realm. The authentic prophet is one who lives primarily a life of prayer. One has to be very disciplined in order to avoid the trap of familiarity.

—Cecelia Williams Bryant

The pastor must develop and operate out of a relevant theological base. If your theology is irrelevant, then your preaching will be irrelevant because it will be done with an irrelevant foundation.

—Jacquelyn Grant

The preacher has to develop the spiritual senses of seeing, hearing, and feeling. God sends a word, and most often that word approaches us. We must be sensitive, open, and cognitive of what is going on around us so that we will receive the word that God is sending to us.

—John R. Bryant

The preacher must have some background as to why the text was written and have some meaningful transitions from the actual reasons why that text was written to how that text applies to the people to whom the preacher is preaching.

—Arthur Brazier

Never leave the congregation on a down note. Always leave them with at least the hope that things will work out. Design the sermon so that the people will leave with the *Good* News.

—Robert Johnson-Smith II

Read yourself full, think yourself clear, pray yourself hot.

—Cecil Bishop

Any good sermon should have inspiration, information, and destination.

—Jesse L. Jackson

Take the time to sit in holy silence to listen to your own spirit, to visualize the faces of your people, and to hear their voices.

—*Arlee Griffin, Jr.*

Make sure that the sermon is clear to you and deeply meaningful for expressing your faith, developing your faith, and convincing others to share your faith.

—*Charles G. Adams*

Make sure that the sermon is biblically grounded.

—*Wyatt Tee Walker*

Take seriously the biblical mandate to pray without ceasing. Be discerning of the generative idea for the sermon in the context of prayer.

—*Robert M. Franklin*

There ought to be the vision of some critical human need that's central within the context of the message itself.

—*Otis Moss, Jr.*

Put in as much time as possible when preparing a sermon.

—*Nelson H. Smith, Jr.*

Preachers must be textual in their approach to the development of the sermon. Let the text speak to the preacher, and let the text speak for itself.

—*James H. Harris*

Start where your people are. Sit where your people sit.

—*Susan D. Newman*

Listen to the sounds and observe the scenes of everyday life.

—*Marshall L. Shepard, Jr.*

Make sure that you are a student of the Bible and do some careful exegesis of what the passage is really saying. Let the message evolve from the passage, rather than superimposing something onto the passage.

—Joseph L. Roberts, Jr.

Gain as much knowledge as you can about what you are going to preach.

—Paul Washington

Preach in series. This will keep you focused and locked into the Scriptures.

—James Hall, Jr.

The sermon should be a three-way dialogue between the preacher, the text, and the Holy Spirit.

—Vashti McKenzie

Read the Scripture passage several times before you consult other resources.

—Evans E. Crawford

Chapter 3

Leading the Sheep
Wisdom on Pastoral Care

The Good Shepherd is our model. Love (agape) is our guiding star. Patience and persistence are our guideposts.

—Joseph E. Lowery

Always be respectful and loving of the people, remembering that if you haven't faced what they are facing, keep living and you will.

—Ralph E. Blanks

Love the people. Let them know that you are available.

—Vashti McKenzie

A pastor must be a preacher, but not every preacher is necessarily a pastor.

—Charles E. Booth

Before a pastor can give pastoral care, he must make sure that he himself is ready and prepared within to render such care. One must make sure that he himself has proper physical, spiritual, and emotional health.

—Michael N. Harris

The undershepherd knows and loves his flock. His compassion should be never-ending.
—*J. Jerome Cooper*

Never be arrogant. Never think that we have the final word or the only answer.
—*Cecil Williams*

Never underestimate the ministry of presence.
—*Susan D. Newman*

The cry of humankind is for someone to love them. Many times, when we approach pastoral care from a "professional" and "psychological" perspective, we lose that human need. As pastors, we must remember that we are not law-givers but lovers.
—*T. Garrott Benjamin, Jr.*

Essentially, pastoral care is showing the love of God in action.
—*Anthony Campbell*

The pastor must keep the strictest confidence.
—*Henry H. Mitchell*

Be prepared to spend another half hour with a person when you are getting ready to leave. You often get to the real issue that people want to discuss when you have your hand on the door, getting ready to leave. Many times everything else is prelude.
—*Beverly J. Shamana*

Love the people. It is important that the pastor does not separate himself or herself from the life experiences of the people. One great danger is that the pastor can become so caught up in the administrative work and in the mechanics of the institution that we lose the heart of the shepherd.
—*Calvin O. Butts III*

Always approach every member out of the depth of creative love, regardless of how unkind that person has been to you, your ministry, or your family.

—*Otis Moss, Jr.*

Visit the sick.

—*Samuel D. Proctor*

When a parishioner calls, never assume that you know what he or she is calling for. Be there to listen and minister to that person in any way you can.

—*Robert Johnson-Smith II*

Be with people in their extremities.

—*Samuel D. Proctor*

Listen to what is behind the words being said. Oftentimes what you hear—that is, the words that are being expressed—is not what people are most concerned about.

—*Beverly Shamana*

The greatest care a pastor can give the sheep and lambs is to feed them a steady diet of the Word of God.

—*Frederick K. C. Price*

Be in touch with the feelings of people.

—*Susan D. Newman*

A pastor must convince the people of his love for them. That is essential because if you don't love the people, you can't help the people. A pastor must have a shepherd's heart. He must convince the people of his concern for their welfare and for their progress in the things of the Spirit, keeping in mind Peter's admonition to grow in grace and in the knowledge of our Lord and Savior, Jesus Christ. Care for the people, because when you identify with the people in the time of crisis, you make a lasting impression for good.

—*Caesar A. W. Clark*

Develop a caring congregation so that caring can be shared.

—*Zan Holmes*

Pastoral care is one of the most important parts of the ministry. It must be done, whether it is by the pastor or by someone designated by the pastor.

—*Mack King Carter*

Listen with the third ear and know when to refer. Everything is not solved by just having a prayer and saying "trust in God."

—*Calvin O. Butts III*

We must suffer with our people.

—*Cecil Williams*

The pastor must go as God's channel for God to speak and heal through the pastor. The person whom the pastor gives care to is God's perfect child. It is the pastor's job and duty to see people as God created them to be, which is perfect and whole. The pastor is there to lift them up and let them know that they are all that God is. They are created out of the body of God; therefore, they are perfect.

—*Johnnie Colemon*

Pastoral care is a twenty-four-hour-a-day, seven-day-a-week occupation.

—*Anthony Campbell*

Pastoral care is essential, but it should be biblically rooted and not guided by secular principles.

—*Frank M. Reid III*

The openness of people to hear you is based on their respect for you.
                                                —*William D. Watley*

Get to know your people by visiting them. Visit under general circumstances, crisis situations, hospital visits, and special counsel sessions.
                                                —*James E. Massey*

You must love people the way Jesus loved people. You must have compassion.
                                                —*Gus Roman*

Love them fully.
                                                —*William A. Jones, Jr.*

Take care of your people. If you don't visit the sick, they will get out of the sick bed and vote you out! The first question people ask when they go to visit someone who is sick is not, "How do your feel?" It is, "Did the pastor come to see you yet?" All of us bear branded on our bodies the stripes of somebody who felt that we did not get there soon enough.
                                                —*Samuel B. McKinney*

The faith that we share is incarnational. Being incarnational creates a scandal of particularity, meaning that God did not come into all races, in all places, at all times. He came into history at a particular place and time, to a particular people and culture. This means that wherever we minister, whether it's the African American community, the Latino community, the Asian community, or the European American community, we have to take the specificity of that culture into context and not be ashamed or embarrassed by that, no more so than God was embarrassed by becoming incarnate in North Africa in the first century. We minister to a specific people at a specific place and time.
                                                —*Jeremiah A. Wright, Jr.*

Know your gifts, and also know those areas that are not your gifts. Know when to refer.

—*Prathia Hall Wynn*

The pastor is the undershepherd and must be sensitive to the needs of the people. As he or she addresses these needs, care should be done with the utmost love and compassion.

—*William B. Moore*

People don't care what you know unless they know you care.

—*Joe S. Ratliff*

The pastor must realize that everyone is carrying a heavy load and is being tried by life. Most people are handling difficult circumstances, known and unknown, with great courage and gallantry. A due respect and admiration for what people are going through belongs to the pastor.

—*Gardner C. Taylor*

The pastor must not be judgmental but be a good listener.

—*J. Deotis Roberts*

Pastors must have a great deal of patience and be willing to extend themselves to look over the flock that God has entrusted to them.

—*Repsie Warren*

Pastors must put themselves in the place of the people they are speaking with, recognizing that what the people need most is someone to love them unconditionally.

—*T. Garrott Benjamin, Jr.*

The pastor must avoid highly directive counseling.

—*Henry H. Mitchell*

Develop a caring attitude throughout the congregation.

—*Emmanuel L. McCall*

The pastor should minister to people in need; then those people who have been ministered to should minister to those who are in a similar need.

—*Johnny Ray Youngblood*

Have a shepherd's heart.

—*J. Wendell Mapson, Jr.*

Love the people whom God has given you to pastor; however, do not become a professional visitor; follow the Word of God and send your deacons.

—*M. Marquette Peace, Jr.*

The life of the pastor must communicate a sense of love for the people he serves. If that shows, the rest of pastoral care is much easier.

—*John H. Adams*

Don't tamper with people's souls. Don't give cheap solutions for problems that require long-range solutions.

—*Katie G. Cannon*

Having a pastor's heart is essential. Unless you ingratiate yourself with your people in their time of need, you have no utilitarian value after the crisis has past. Everyone falls in love with the nurse, so the pastor must be there to heal.

—*Cecil Murray*

Maintain the strictest confidentiality.

—*Corneilius Henderson*

Pastoral care should be provided with compassion along with a critical look at the situation when it is necessary.

—Sherman G. Hicks

Do not air the dirty linen of your members during a sermon.

—Ella P. Mitchell

God has already done everything in time and eternity. It is up to us to apply what God has done to the lives of people.

—Benjamin Smith

Love the people.

—Alvin O. Jackson

Listen to the presented problem, but focus on the real problem. Listen, observe, and feel wholistically.

—David T. Shannon

Without letting it stifle us, we must be aware of the fact that people are looking to us for their own care and the improvement of others.

—Frank B. Mitchell, Jr.

Pastoral care is basic in a successful pastorate. The congregation must know that the pastor is available.

—Robert Johnson-Smith, Sr.

The pastor should give options rather than direct advice.

—J. Deotis Roberts

Love the people. It is hard to pastor or even preach without *really* caring for the people.

—Manuel L. Scott, Sr.

Pastoral care happens throughout worship, daily life, and through relationships with people. It is not just hospital visitation. Pastoral care provides leadership and guidance to those whom we serve.

—William E. Hayman, Jr.

Pastoral care creates the bonding with the congregation. The sharing of experiences, both the valleys and the mountain peaks, creates the trust that is so vitally needed for the people and their pastor.

—Delores Carpenter

Use a team ministry in pastoral care, knowing that any representative from the church is a representative of the pastor. The congregation must be taught to receive representatives of the church other than the pastor.

—Suzan Johnson Cook

Be sensitive to the total needs of the parishioner.

—Corneilius Henderson

Every pastor, to be successful, must be a lover of people. If the pastor is not a lover of people, he must work to cultivate that sensitive emotion to learn to care for people and their needs.

—T. J. Jemison, Sr.

Make sure that you love God and that you love his people. Make no distinction in people because of socio-economic levels.

—E. Edward Jones

Through compassionate pastoral care, you knit the souls of the people together, as well as knit them to yourself.

—James C. Perkins

It is important for the pastor to apply scriptural principles to daily living, having been led by the Holy Spirit.

—*Benjamin Smith*

Every pastor should have a shepherd's heart, a love towards the flock, especially the weak and those who need it the most.

—*Thomas Kilgore, Jr.*

Pray for wisdom and insight so that you know what the needs of people really are.

—*Joy Clark*

Involve as many people as possible in the ministry of pastoral care, making every effort to properly equip them to do so. The pastor must equip carers.

—*William J. Shaw*

A preacher once told me that if we do not have time for our people, our people will not have time for us. The essence of pastoral care is not so much psychological or theological. The essence of pastoral care is care. The pastor must care about what happens to the people, must care about how and why they hurt, and must care enough to listen to what they have to say. Pastoral care requires care.

—*H. Beecher Hicks, Jr.*

Be honest with the person you are engaging in pastoral care.

—*James H. Evans, Jr.*

As you minister to others, make sure that you and your family are ministered to somewhere.

—*Suzan Johnson Cook*

The pastor should not launch immediately into what may appear to be the problem. The pastor should find some common ground with the parishioner that has nothing to do with the problem but draws them together. The pastor must go from the known to the unknown.

—Joseph Roberts

Think of how Jesus would handle the situation.

—Marshall L. Shepard, Jr.

Be compassionate towards all of the people.

—James H. Harris

Every pastor should know himself or herself. The best way to come to understand oneself is to have clinical pastoral education and, if one can afford it, go into personal therapy for at least a year. You will learn a great deal about yourself. If you come out all right, everyone else will come out all right.

—Lawrence E. Carter, Sr.

Take time to listen.

—Dennis W. Wiley

Learn the technique of taking care of people within social structures.

—Forrest Harris

The pastor does not necessarily have to have solutions to people's problems, but the pastor must be present at the time of need.

—Wallace C. Smith

A pastor must be mindful of his or her sense of call. There must be a love for the profession and a love for the people served. All of this stems from the original love that one has for God.

—G. Daniel Jones

Know when the counseling is beyond your professional scope. Be able to suggest other resources for your client.

—Jesse Brown, Jr.

Be real.

—Mack H. Smith

Real pastoral care grows out of a pastor's genuine love for people.

—Albert Campbell

Know your limitations. God does not call us to fix people. God calls us to walk with people in their time of need.

—H. Dean Trulear

Know the people as much as you can. Make sure that you offer the type of pastoral care that you would need and want for yourself.

—J. Wendell Mapson, Sr.

Love God's people.

—Maurice Green

Visit the sick.

—Sara Potter Smith

Help the people to know each other. The members of the congregation should minister to each other, just as the pastor ministers to the congregation. The pastor is the example or guide on how care is to be given.

—James E. Massey

The pastor must develop and operate out of a relevant theological base. If your theology is irrelevant, then your pastoral care will be irrelevant because it will be done with an irrelevant foundation.

—Jacquelyn Grant

The pastor must be available for the people. —*Floyd Massey*

Integrity in ministry is dependent on the prophet having discerned and owned her own broken places and offered them over to the Lord. Also, when required, the prophet should pursue godly therapy so that when the prophet ministers from her broken places, believers are not made subject to her but to the grace of God.

—*Cecelia Williams Bryant*

"Do unto others as you would have them do unto you." Try to walk in the shoes of others in society and respond to them the way you would want to be responded to. —*John R. Bryant*

Pastors must do everything they can to make themselves available to the people for pastoral counseling. —*Arthur Brazier*

Relate openly with your people. Be yourself among them and seek to know as much as possible about them so that you can help them to be themselves. —*James E. Massey*

Know the flock and love them. —*Cecil Bishop*

Pastoral care is the foundation on which a faithful ministry is built. It is the glue that holds the relationship between pastor and people together. —*Arlee Griffin, Jr.*

Always make the person central to the process. We have to be totally committed to the care of the person and not simply to the carrying out of a process. —*Charles G. Adams*

Take care of the old folks and the young folks.
—Wyatt Tee Walker

Recognize your limits as a pastoral caregiver.
—Robert M. Franklin

Pastoral ministry is a two-way street. Sometimes the pastor receives as much or more from the pastoral care experience than the one being cared for.
—Paul Washington

The pastor must have a shepherd's heart not only in terms of the congregation but also in terms of the community.
—Wallace S. Hartsfield

Every person in the congregation needs pastoral care: men, women, boys, girls, old, young, rich, and poor. They all need to know that somebody cares.
—Catherine I. Godboldte

Chapter 4

The Moses Dilemma
Wisdom on Church Administration

The church is a theocracy and not a democracy.
—Olin P. Moyd

Find someone who can do administration. The day of the pastor doing everything is over.
—Cecil Williams

Never require of your employees anything that you do not exhibit in your own lifestyle.
—Susan D. Newman

Remember that the pastor is ultimately responsible for everything that comes forth from his desk.
—J. Wendell Mapson, Jr.

Before you reach for the whip, take hold of the reins. Many pastors take the whip and try to whip people in line before they take control of the reigns. If you have the reins in your hands, you may not need the whip.
—Samuel B. McKinney

Our success as pastors rises or falls, sinks or swims, on our ability as administrators.
—Bennett W. Smith, Sr.

For the new pastor, church administration is knowing what not to do.
—*Anthony Campbell*

Don't sign the checks.
—*Henry H. Mitchell*

Never assume that you have all of the answers and all of the strategies. Always know that there are persons among us and around us with skills, abilities, and insights who, in most instances, are willing to share them, without arrogance or even credit.
—*Otis Moss, Jr.*

Learn as much about business administration as you can. If the pastor cannot handle the administration, he or she needs to have people around who can.
—*Katie G. Cannon*

You can't do it by yourself.
—*Delores Carpenter*

The key to most administrative problems in the visible kingdom is what happens at preaching time on Sunday morning.
—*William A. Jones, Jr.*

Whatever you do, preach. If you do not preach, you will have nothing to administer.
—*Samuel B. McKinney*

Take the responsibility seriously. Be accountable for all of your actions and decisions. Learn how to delegate tasks to others. Let everything you do be done decently and in order.
—*J. Jerome Cooper*

Clergypersons going into the twenty-first century have to be aware of the fact that excellent business skills are as important as finely tuned exegetical skills. It is mandatory in terms of good stewardship to know business principles.

—Jeremiah A. Wright, Jr.

Keep the best records that you can, starting with day one of your pastorate.

—Ralph E. Blanks

A pastor can run the church or run around in it. If the pastor does not have administrative skills, he should make people the object of his ministry and use their skills.

—Joe S. Ratliff

Learn how to delegate.

—Susan D. Newman

The pastor must make sure that the lines of communication are crystal clear.

—G. Daniel Jones

Don't try to do it all yourself. Don't think you know everything about running the church. Rely on people around you for counsel.

—Leon H. Sullivan

A church has to have a shepherd who is able to administer "tough love." An administration without love is hard and cold, while an administration that shows love only will probably show some weakness in development.

—T. Garrott Benjamin, Jr.

Make use of the latest technology. Do not be afraid to be creatively new. Let your administration be designed for reaching ends. It should not just be traditional. It should be pointed and be moving in a specific direction.

—Emmanuel L. McCall

The church must look to the Bible to take care of the church as opposed to the methods of other types of organizations. The church is a corpus, while other organizations are corpses.

—Johnny Ray Youngblood

Pay attention to details.

—J. Wendell Mapson, Jr.

Train the laypeople and delegate responsibility.

—Ella P. Mitchell

Your administrative ability is shown by how well you train your people and designate responsibilities. Ask for excellence: God's church should show the world how it's done.

—M. Marquette Peace, Jr.

Get as much additional training as you can in administration, over and beyond that which the church and the seminary provide.

—John H. Adams

Judgments of the head should emanate from love of the people in the heart.

—Joseph E. Lowery

Caesar Clark once told me that there is a difference between a problem and a situation. You can solve a problem, but a situation has to work itself out.

—Anthony Campbell

Unless you take care of the details of operation, you will soon have no operation to take care of.

—Cecil Murray

Administration in the church is management of people and

resources. It should be done with the utmost care. It is the activity that ties all of the work of the church together. Therefore there should be a clear sense of purpose, direction, and goals, so that the work of the kingdom gets done, through people, to the glory of God.

—*William B. Moore*

Study the activities of the most successful church administrators and extrapolate from that study those habits, skills, and endowments that have led them to be where they are.

—*Corneilius Henderson*

Be sure you have adequate bylaws and regular audits.

—*Samuel D. Proctor*

While it is important, it should not keep the pastor glued behind the desk.

—*Beverly J. Shamana*

Administrate by following the Great Administrator, the Holy Spirit.

—*Frederick K. C. Price*

The pastor must go in advance of the people without detaching himself from the people. He must keep in mind that the people may not be able to walk as quickly or as rapidly as he would like to lead them. He must keep away from forcing the issue and forcing people to move at a speed for which they are not equipped in this day and time. Many a great church has been torn up by young, ambitious men who wanted to carry the people faster than the people were capable of going.

—*Caesar A. W. Clark*

Pastors must determine if they have gifts in administration. The pastor must also be very clear on whether administration means being a dictator or whether it means being someone who

assembles a team to get the job done. The bottom line of church administration is to get the job done.
—*Mack King Carter*

Work with your officers. God does not give the pastor everything. You may be able to preach, but you may not understand all of the details of running that particular church. You may be a good judge of character, but you may not handle money well. Learn to surround yourself with the best and the brightest, those people who may be smarter than you in their line of work, who love the Lord.
—*Calvin O. Butts III*

It's all right to be friends with your employees as well as their supervisor or boss.
—*Susan D. Newman*

The church must reflect responsible, disciplined, and accountable leadership.
—*Charles E. Booth*

It is important for the pastor to be the chief executive officer while at the same time learning to delegate responsibility. So many pastors are suffering from burnout because they attempt to do it all. The pastor must develop an appreciation for the body of Christ and the ability to attract, train, and nurture the gifts and talents of other ministerial staff persons, laypersons, and employees.
—*Fred A. Lucas, Jr.*

While the pastor has the game plan, he or she must realize that pastors do not have to carry the ball on every play. The pastor must be able to pass the ball from time to time.
—*J. Alfred Smith, Sr.*

Pastors must be absolutely certain that they are at the church that the Lord directed them to. If pastors are at the church where

the Lord wants them to be, then the Lord wants them to be at that church for a particular reason. The pastor's administration program will grow out of this relationship.
—*Michael N. Harris*

We do ourselves and the lay leadership of our churches a great disservice when we try to administrate the church in the same way that we administer our businesses.
—*Frank M. Reid III*

Make sure those in leadership feel that they have something to say about what is going on in the church.
—*Floyd Massey, Jr.*

Find a way of delegating responsibility to other people.
—*Sherman G. Hicks*

Keep your leaders abreast of any changes in your plan. Constantly be in dialogue with your leaders.
—*Ella P. Mitchell*

Next to a strong biblical background, church administration is the single most important aspect of the pastorate.
—*Bennett W. Smith, Sr.*

Pastors must observe the people around them, especially those who volunteer their services to the Lord. Pastors must examine their motives for service. If there are no ulterior motives, pastors must then look at the résumé of each person to see where his or her talent lies. These persons should be put in places of service, and authority should be delegated to them. They should then be supervised by the pastor.
—*Benjamin Smith*

You must have a competent staff.
—*Delores Carpenter*

The pastor/preacher should be a person of basic integrity when it comes to money. He ought to press for openness and accountability with a budgetary system of operations. While the pastor maintains the general oversight, he should not be the handler of the monies.
—*Manuel L. Scott, Sr.*

Focus upon goal and outcome; then determine strategies and tactics.
—*David T. Shannon, Sr.*

The people need openness. They need to know what we are doing.
—*Frank B. Mitchell, Jr.*

The pastor must know the leadership abilities of his people and should use the people who are resourceful in certain areas in the structure of the administration.
—*Robert Johnson-Smith, Sr.*

Pastors must surround themselves with people who have gifts in administration. But in order to do this, pastors must have confidence in themselves.
—*Alvin O. Jackson*

Church administration is a two-edged sword. While you should give as much as you can, you must not get tied down to administrative tasks.
—*William E. Hayman, Jr.*

Do not procrastinate. Do it right away.
—*Delores Carpenter*

Keep everything on top of the table, according to vote.
—*Henry H. Mitchell*

Do not take people by surprise. As the child psychologists

have pointed out, a large part of an infant's terror is shock due to jerking or sudden movement. People need to be prepared for every step we make. A great deal of our trouble comes from shocking people and not giving them a chance to let things sink in.

—Gardner C. Taylor

The pastor must be the leader of the administration while working cooperatively with the official boards.

—T. J. Jemison, Sr.

Take seriously the business aspects of the kingdom's work and proceed with that work as if you had invested your last dime in a venture of your own.

—E. Edward Jones

Whenever possible, build a team ministry. Build a team around you that has strengths that you do not have, and have the confidence to respect them as professionals. Delegate when necessary. Schedule time to do administrative tasks. Good time management is essential.

—Suzan Johnson Cook

The administration of the church should grow out of whatever the pastor and people perceive the mission of the church to be.

—James C. Perkins

Effective administration frees you up to do ministry. Sloppy administration bogs you down and prevents you from doing ministry.

—Cain Hope Felder

Pray for wisdom, and tithe.

—Joy Clark

Govern with an iron fist and a velvet glove.

—Susan D. Newman

Tailor your administrative design not only to what the church desires but also to what you are comfortable with.

—*Charles E. Booth*

Find a competent administrative assistant.

—*Dennis W. Wiley*

The larger a church becomes, the more important it is for the minister to find a way to seek out training in business and management. Those who do not have these skills can become crippled as they go the method of trial and error. Get training, get training, get training!

—*H. Beecher Hicks, Jr.*

Always be fair and above board in every decision that you make and in every action that you undertake.

—*James H. Evans, Jr.*

While having a solid foundation in business and management principles is extremely important, it is imperative that we recognize that we are *participating* in leading a spiritual business.

—*Frank M. Reid III*

Stay on top of it [church administration]. If you can't do it effectively, get someone who can. Whomever you get should love the Lord, be competent, and be personally committed to the pastor.

—*William D. Watley*

You must understand the needs of the people and how best to meet those needs. You must know how to organize people to meet those needs.

—*Gus Roman*

While administration is important, pastors must not get

bogged down in doing things that they do not have to do. Pastors should arrange their offices so that capable people are able to do many administrative tasks, so that they as pastors are free to do those tasks they and only they can do.
—*Vashti McKenzie*

The pastor must listen before he or she speaks.
—*Joseph L. Roberts, Jr.*

A church is spiritual, but it is also a business. The church must be handled as a business in terms of keeping records and holding the necessary meetings. The church is God's organization, and there should be nothing but harmony, divine order, and peace.
—*Johnnie Colemon*

Utilize the characteristics of sympathy, harmony, vision, and the companionship of the Holy Spirit.
—*Marshall L. Shepard, Jr.*

If one looks closely at the modern principles of administration and management, one will find that most of them are rooted in Scripture.
—*Frank M. Reid III*

The pastor must provide leadership. This is the critical issue.
—*James H. Harris*

The corporate setting must be kept out of the church. The Bible offers us guidelines as to how the church should be run.
—*Nelson H. Smith, Jr.*

If you are not a good administrator, find someone in your church who is.
—*Aidsand Wright-Riggins*

Find a way to equip yourself administratively.

—*Dennis W. Wiley*

Surround yourself with a good staff of experts.

—*Forrest Harris*

You must have good record keeping so that you can account for whatever the people are doing, or giving, or sharing with the church. The people need to have accountability because they are the ones who are supporting the church financially.

—*Johnnie Colemon*

The pastor must develop a serious teaching ministry within the church. The people cannot be blamed for what they have not been taught.

—*James H. Harris*

The pastor must build a climate in the church where people feel good about doing church work.

—*Wallace C. Smith*

As a pastor, one must be the leader in coordinating a team effort.

—*G. Daniel Jones*

Let the laypeople of the church do most of the church administration.

—*Jesse Brown, Jr.*

Church administration is something you learn by jumping into the fire.

—*Mack H. Smith*

Church administration is always in flux in the sense that one is always learning the process and learning from the process.

There are few rules of thumb because of the diversity of church life.
                                                    —*Albert Campbell*

Always look through the program to the people.
                                                    —*H. Dean Trulear*

No organization, no group, no church can go beyond the consciousness of its leader.
                                                    —*Johnnie Colemon*

The pastor must see administration in terms of ministry. Any well-organized church runs the risk of becoming so bureaucratized that it loses sight of the servant goals and of the people.
                                                    —*H. Dean Trulear*

The pastor should know where the people are at a given time and know where he is trying to lead them. Administrative efforts should be in the direction of elevating the people. We are in the business of transformation. Whatever we do, we should try to help people fulfill their dreams so that they can be the people that God wants them to be.
                                                    —*L. Vencheal Booth*

Know the structure and operation of the church's life. Guide it, but do not attempt to control it.
                                                    —*James E. Massey*

The pastor must develop and operate out of a relevant theological base. If your theology is irrelevant, then your church administration will be irrelevant because it will be done with an irrelevant foundation.
                                                    —*Jacquelyn Grant*

Don't worry about who gets the credit.
                                                    —*Floyd Massey, Jr.*

The person who has the vision for the ministry is not often or always the person who has the gifts of administration. One has to be able to emotionally extract oneself and one's ego from the process in order to maintain integrity and accountability as a part of the administration. It is the prophet's responsibility to make sure that there is solidarity in the process.

—Cecelia Williams Bryant

The pastor must be accountable.

—John R. Bryant

If the pastor brings on an administrator, that person should be a Christian and a member of the church.

—Arthur Brazier

Do what you must do in terms of administration, but always leave the people with their dignity.

—Robert Johnson-Smith II

Know as much as you can, but be willing to share with others in the leadership process.

—Cecil Bishop

Seek to be efficient, but most importantly, be effective.

—Arlee Griffin, Jr.

Be honest, be accountable, be faithful.

—Charles G. Adams

The staff must understand the consciousness of its church's leader. Once they understand what the leader is all about, then the staff must follow the leader.

—Johnnie Colemon

The operation of the church should be done in a professional, organized, and efficient manner at all times.
—Vashti McKenzie

The pastor must be collegial in the area of church administration. The pastor cannot be a dictator. There must be a sense of participatory government.
—Wyatt Tee Walker

The pastor must always know the subpolitical structure in the church. Look at the formal structure and the informal structure of the church.
—Joseph L. Roberts, Jr.

Get people around you who can do the work that needs to be done to minister to the needs of the people.
—James Hall, Jr.

Keep the channels of communication open with the congregation. People like to know what is going on in their church. Enable the congregation to participate in the life of the church.
—Catherine I. Godboldte

Chapter 5

Voices to the Future
Wisdom to Those Who Are Just Beginning

Love the people wherever you find them, whenever you find them. Never be found guilty of not doing your work.

—*Ralph E. Blanks*

Be wise as a serpent and gentle as a dove. Have a great deal of patience and a sense of humor.

—*Renita J. Weems*

Get to know the people. Go slow with them. Love them.

—*Alvin O. Jackson*

Benjamin E. Mays once said, "Before you use your influence, you should have it."

—*Robert Johnson-Smith, Sr.*

Many young pastors today are concerned with fleecing the flock and not feeding the flock. A pastor must have a shepherd's heart.

—*Charles E. Booth*

Remember that you are there to serve the congregation.

—*James H. Evans, Jr.*

Forget your program and concentrate on the people. If you

are able to concentrate on the people and bring them to a point where they have confidence in who you are and what you are doing, then implementation of your program will become a matter of course. If you put program in front of people, the resistance will be incredible, and the ministry will be frustrating.

—*H. Beecher Hicks, Jr.*

Do not rush, but have a deep respect for the church and its history. Build on people's sense of self rather than trying to change that sense of self.

—*William J. Shaw*

Be yourself. Develop your own style of preaching. You cannot be someone else. Be sure you have your values intact, and be impeccably honest.

—*Thomas Kilgore, Jr.*

Give the church as much concentrated time as possible.

—*Cain Hope Felder*

Learn and respect the wants, needs, aspirations, and history of the people before you make any decisions.

—*Olin P. Moyd*

Find out where the people are. Lead them gradually.

—*James C. Perkins*

Be mentored by those who have already been through what you're getting ready to go through. Realize that the seminary is only part of your preparation and that there are certain things that only pastoring can teach you.

—*Suzan Johnson Cook*

Observe very closely what is going on before making any changes.

—*E. Edward Jones*

Do not take sides with people who did or did not vote for you. Do not even try to find out who they were. Stay in the biblical role, preach the gospel, and take care of the needs of all of the people. By doing this, you will win those you did not have and keep those you do have.

—T. J. Jemison, Sr.

Spend the first year listening.

—Delores Carpenter

When the pastor is convinced that God has called him or her to a particular church, he or she should go into it with a long-haul view.

—William B. Moore

Do your homework. Take the job seriously. If you're in it for the duration, don't be in a rush. Pray on it.

—William E. Hayman, Jr.

The call itself and acceptance of the call does not make you a pastor. A new pastor should realize that he shouldn't pop his whip if he hasn't got it in his hand. If he hasn't got his hand on the steering wheel, he should not turn the corner. A new pastor should just preach and pray for quite a while.

—Manuel L. Scott, Sr.

It is an illusion to think that you have become pastor because you have become settled. You pastor only those who know and hear your voice.

—Manuel L. Scott, Sr.

Remember who you are and who called you to this ministry. Learn how to love and respect the people under your care.

—J. Jerome Cooper

It's all about growing. You must stay very close with God. You have to listen to and talk to God. The difficult part is that you have nobody you can really talk to, so you have to get accustomed to talking to God, listening to God, and then obeying God.

—*Johnnie Colemon*

Take advantage of the honeymoon period.

—*Alvin O. Jackson*

Young pastors should read about the lives of outstanding pastors who have had distinguished careers as pastors.

—*Frank B. Mitchell, Jr.*

Ask God for wisdom, strength, and guidance.

—*David T. Shannon*

As a new pastor, you must be absolutely sure of your calling. You must have the mind of the great Shepherd while understanding that you are the undershepherd, under the direction of God's executive director, the Holy Spirit.

—*Benjamin Smith*

Don't start doing something that you can't keep up.

—*Bennett W. Smith, Sr.*

Take your time, learn the people. Understand what they are thinking and feeling, and meet their needs. Find out where the people are and move them, with some gradual understanding of their needs, to where you want them to go.

—*Ella P. Mitchell*

Through being attentive to the flock, you earn the right to be heard by your people.

—*James C. Perkins*

Love your people. If you do not love your people, you cannot be a shepherd.
—*Sherman G. Hicks*

Study the congregation and the community. Know the demographics.
—*Wallace S. Hartsfield*

Go with a sense of humility. Go with a sense of mission. Go with a sense of assurance in terms of calling, commitment, and dependence on the grace of God.
—*Otis Moss, Jr.*

Understand that man looks at the outside, but God sees the inside . . . and soon, people will see both.
—*Joseph E. Lowery*

When you are called to a church to be the pastor, the church is simply giving you a *chance* to be pastor. You are not the pastor the day you walk in. You are not the pastor because you have a reserved parking space. You are not the pastor because you have a set of keys to the church. Remember that the person who painted your name on the door can paint it off. You have to *become* the pastor.
—*Anthony Campbell*

Don't change anything in your first year.
—*Susan D. Newman*

Do not feel that you must make significant changes in the first week or the first month.
—*Cecil Williams*

Learn lessons from respected pastors.
—*Michael N. Harris*

Never go one-on-one with a person at the time of controversy. Stay on the principle and not on the principal.
—*Cecil Murray*

Stay with the Bible. Stay with principles. Don't let anyone pull you off of what you really believe.
—*Johnnie Colemon*

Never underestimate the power of wisdom in the pew. The person who appears to be the most ignorant in the congregation knows when you've flunked!
—*Otis Moss, Jr.*

The late Dr. Sandy Ray taught me that a pastor is like the steam engine of a freight train that has to back up and hook up his cars. Once you have hooked up your cars, you can roll.
—*J. Alfred Smith, Sr.*

Be prepared to struggle and sacrifice. Many leave the seminary with a master's degree, expecting the benefits, gratification, and salary commensurate with their level of training. In most cases, in the black church, that is not going to be the case. It is important to go in with a mind to work and build and be proud yet humble. A pastor must bloom where he or she is planted. Leadership should be patient, progressive, bold, visionary, creative, spiritual, and socially committed.
—*Fred A. Lucas, Jr.*

Take time and study your people to determine what the spiritual climate is. No pastor should go into a pastorate with a predetermined program. This is a setup for failure. It is ecclesiastical suicide.
—*Charles E. Booth*

Take time to preach well, often. Visit the sick and care for the affairs of the church. Don't try to run the community and the world right away. Don't do what you've seen the "old" pastors do. Learn your congregation. Work closely to establish yourself in conjunction with who the people are. In other words, you cannot do in your first year what Sandy Ray did after being in a church for thirty years.

—Calvin O. Butts III

Remember that it takes a long time to become pastor. Though you are given the title "pastor," you're really not. You must prove yourself.

—Mack King Carter

A young pastor should go into a church loving God supremely and loving the people truly. The young pastor should keep in mind that of all the things a pastor may not have, the one thing that he must have is patience.

—Caesar A. W. Clark

Find out what *God* called you to do and don't deviate from it.

—Frederick K. C. Price

Be ready to learn from the congregation. Listen and hear what the people are dealing with.

—Beverly J. Shamana

Follow Jesus. Jesus gives the example of sincerity, simplicity, humility, and trust.

—Samuel D. Proctor

Serve God by putting God first, your family second, and your job third. By all means, serve the Lord with jubilation, effervescence, and total commitment. Love the people unapologetically.

—Corneilius Henderson

Develop good study habits.

—Lawrence E. Carter, Sr.

Remember that you are neither the first nor the last leader that your congregation will ever have, but it may be your first and last assignment.
—Otis Moss, Jr.

Find yourself a close-knit cadre of caring, thinking, loyal persons who can help you take ownership of the vision you have for the church and thus sell it to the larger congregation.
—Cecil Murray

A pastor should have one ear on the ground, listening to the cries and longings of the people, and the other ear at the mouth of God.
—Katie G. Cannon

Seek the counsel of a seasoned pastor to get guidance on how to enter a new congregation for the first time.
—John H. Adams

Incorporate the biblical principles of pastoring. "The Holy Ghost has made you overseers"; no one should pastor for you. Yet never neglect "feeding the flock of God."
—M. Marquette Peace, Jr.

Spend some time learning the congregation's history before making any abrupt changes.
—J. Wendell Mapson, Jr.

Take your time and get to know your people. Let the program be determined by the needs of the people and the opportunities that are available.
—Emmanuel McCall

Pray, pray, pray.
—Repsie Warren

Do not go into your first pastorate believing that you know

everything. Listen to the people and learn from them also. Then, with your education, advice from others, and your will to continue to learn, you will be going in the direction of becoming an effective pastor.

—*Leon H. Sullivan*

Pastors must be available for the direction of God. Alexander McClaren called it "sitting silent before God." Pastors must seek God's will for their lives and be available for what God wants them to do.

—*Gardner C. Taylor*

Do not go in with a preplanned program that you want to sell. Get to know your people; get to know the issues.

—*J. Deotis Roberts*

A new pastor should spend a lot of time studying his situation. He must be prayerful for a vision for that church. He should take the skills learned in seminary and see how they can be used in that particular place. He should try to impress the people who are present in the church and not so much those who are outside the church.

—*Joe S. Ratliff*

Be an interpreter of the deep, timeless issues of human existence.

—*Amos Brown*

A new pastor should remember that he or she is a graft into a congregation that has a personality, a history, problems, and potential. As with all new organisms grafted into an already-existing organism, it takes time for the graft to take. The new pastor must learn the people, their history, their problems, their fears, and their strengths. You must become one of them before you can start to make radical changes.

—*Jeremiah A. Wright, Jr.*

Don't preach your doubts. Preach your certainties—that is, what you believe and what you know to be real.

—Samuel B. McKinney

When your "enemies" in the congregation acknowledge you as pastor, then you are indeed the pastor of that church.

—Michael N. Harris

God will send you people who need to be fed. In order to feed them, you must prepare yourself to feed them. If you give the people a good meal and if you prepare a good feast, they will be back because they like the food that you are feeding them.

—Johnnie Colemon

Make preaching your preeminent priority.

—William A. Jones, Jr.

Pray, listen. Pray, listen. Pray, listen. Pray, listen.

—Gus Roman

Break the fifty-dollar bills of theology, philosophy, and church history into the dollar, fifty cents, quarter, dime, nickel, and penny currencies of the laity.

—Amos Brown

Preach the gospel, love the people, and pace yourself.

—William D. Watley

Stay focused on the primary mission, which is to be the spokesperson and God's representative to his people. Don't let anyone or anything sway you from your calling.

—Repsie Warren

The wisdom of pastoring is knowing what changes you can make immediately and what changes take a little more time.

—Wyatt Tee Walker

Go to a university in the area and get a degree that allows you to do research on some phase of the history of your church or church life in that community. *—Samuel B. McKinney*

Learn how to organize your personal life. Time management is crucial. *—Frank M. Reid III*

Love the people, and the rest will follow. *—Vashti Mckenzie*

You will be more effective by living sermons than by delivering sermons. *—Paul Washington*

Be acutely aware of the things you must unlearn. *—Marshall L. Shepard, Jr.*

Be open-minded. Be willing to learn the culture of that particular congregation. *—James H. Harris*

Listen to the stories of the elders of your church. *—Robert M. Franklin*

Listen and hear the *needs* of the people. *—Frank M. Reid III*

Come to the assignment with the understanding that it is a divine assignment. Remember that we do not have ownership of

the ministry, nor do we have ownership of the people who are entrusted to our charge. We are assigned to them, but ultimately, they belong to God.
                                              —*Prathia Hall Wynn*

Don't try to change the world overnight.
                                              —*Dennis W. Wiley*

Have your study arranged so that you are literally growing a garden of sermons all at once. You will discover that they all do not mature or blossom at the same time, but you will be watering, hoeing, and cultivating quite a few.
                                              —*Lawrence E. Carter, Sr.*

Allow people to initiate and make some changes.
                                              —*Ella P. Mitchell*

If you concentrate on your problems, you can't enjoy your blessings.
                                              —*Dennis W. Wiley*

Take the time to reflect upon the history that is there [at the church] to be learned. Take time to reflect upon the people who remain as a part of that history.
                                              —*Forrest Harris*

Develop the spiritual disciplines: prayer, fasting, and Scripture reading.
                                              —*Frank M. Reid III*

Try to keep a written agenda for all meetings and to cling to that agenda, or you will find yourself far afield.
                                              —*Cecil Murray*

Make every effort to hear the congregation's stories. Spend a significant time just listening.
                                              —*Wallace C. Smith*

The pastorate is difficult work. It led Jesus to Calvary. But for every crucifixion, there's a resurrection.

—*Fred A. Lucas, Jr.*

The new pastor must realize that if he or she has been called to a church, the people had a church before he or she arrived. They have a history, they have a togetherness, and they have a bond. They do not have a bond with the new pastor yet. As he or she ministers to the flock, bonding takes place, and when bonding takes place, the atmosphere is set for extended and expanded ministry.

—*G. Daniel Jones*

Listen to everyone, but don't let people tell you what to do; that's God's job.

—*Michael N. Harris*

Be creative in your ministry.

—*Jesse Brown, Jr.*

Don't trust the first people who run to your face to tell you that they are going to be in your corner.

—*Mack H. Smith*

Take your time, but don't take your time. Some things need to be changed immediately, but it takes time for changes to take place. Be alert and sensitive to the need for change, but also be alert and sensitive to the process of change.

—*Albert Campbell*

Get to know the people.

—*H. Dean Trulear*

Take time to survey your congregation. Find out what the needs are and meet those needs.

—*J. Wendell Mapson, Sr.*

Don't make any changes fast. Get to know the people.

—*Maurice Green*

The pastorate must be approached prayerfully. There must be a dependency on God for empowerment, for motivation, and for effectiveness.

—*G. Daniel Jones*

Write out every sermon, word for word.

—*Lawrence E. Carter, Sr.*

Be ambitionless so that the will of God for that people can flow through you.

—*Cecelia Williams Bryant*

Try to bring the ideal and real together.

—*L. Venchael Booth*

Learn the heritage and previous leadership of the congregation that you seek to serve.

—*James E. Massey*

Programs are secondary to building relationships in the church.

—*G. Daniel Jones*

Be willing to adjust your expectations after a fairly short time of doing ministry.

—*Jesse Brown, Jr.*

Be open to learn as you lead. Learn from the people as you lead them.

—*James E. Massey*

Go with an open mind to listen and to learn. Go prepared to teach.

—Jacquelyn Grant

Pay tribute to your predecessor if that person was of good character.

—Floyd Massey, Jr.

Ask God for an unconditional love for the people you were sent to minister to.

—Cecelia Williams Bryant

Struggle to love the people. Work to keep love alive between pastor and people, just as you would work to keep love alive between husband and wife.

—John R. Bryant

Pray for an understanding heart so that you might be able to serve the people.

—L. Venchael Booth

Curb impetuosity.

—Arthur Brazier

Seek to be faithful in meeting the needs of the people in the areas of pastoral care, preaching, and administration. When you are faithful in these areas, you can build your ministry in any direction you choose, based on this foundation.

—Arlee Griffin

Take your time. Don't make changes too swiftly. Find out where you are, with whom you are dealing, and what their history has been. Study the situation for at least twelve months before proposing any major changes in any aspect of the church's life.

—Charles G. Adams

When you get to a church, do not be overly concerned about who is in charge. During the first year or so, just preach the gospel.

—Wyatt Tee Walker

Find an experienced mentor with whom you can share your questions and your struggles.

—James E. Massey

Remember that the people need you, but also remember that you need the people in order to be the pastor you want to be.

—L. Venchael Booth

Remember the old saying: "All men stand on the shoulders of other men."

—Nelson H. Smith, Jr.

Be yourself.

—Catherine I. Godboldte

Chapter 6

Voices from the Past
Wisdom from Those Who Have Gone On

A people without a history of itself is like a tree without roots.
—*The late Joshua E. Licorish to Ralph E. Blanks*

Pastor your church as if you are going to be at that church forever, but be ready to leave in twenty-four hours.
—*The late J. H. L. Smith to Robert Johnson-Smith II*

The pastor must respect the people he serves.
—*The late Sandy Ray to Olin P. Moyd*

Keep the faith, no matter what the circumstances may be.
—*The late Massie Kennard to Sherman G. Hicks*

The pastor must be cautious and not embrace too quickly those who are in leadership positions. These people must be studied and kept at arm's length until the pastor has prayed and the Lord has revealed to them the type of people they truly are. These people may turn on the pastor and, if they have been close to the pastor, they can do greater damage.
—*The late Martin Luther King, Sr., to Bennett W. Smith, Sr.*

If a pastor wants to have power in his ministry, the pastor must have a strong prayer life.
—The late A. H. Anderson to Thomas Kilgore, Jr.

Pastors should learn to master time and never be in a hurry.
—The late Erick Herrick to Robert Johnson-Smith, Sr.

"And it came to pass." No matter what it is that we are going through, it is going to pass, whether it's good, bad, or indifferent.
—The late Robert Peoples to Alvin O. Jackson

There is power and significance in the humility of the preacher. The privacy of preaching is the pastor's work. The one thing that the pastor can do that no one else in the church can do is preach. That is not given to the laity, no matter how eloquently they can talk. The preacher can get more done with his preaching than with any politicking.
—The late Sandy Ray to Manuel L. Scott, Sr.

Always love the people and preach biblical sermons. Do not get into the personal lives of the people unless they invite you in.
—The late D. V. Jemison, Sr., to T. J. Jemison, Sr.

The pastor must care for and identify with the needs of the people of the congregation. The pastor must be there when the people need him or her. Pastors must be true to their calling.
—The late J. H. L. Smith to Robert Johnson-Smith, Sr.

Ministers are human.
—The late Eugene Houston to Suzan Johnson Cook

Tend to the needs of the flock . . . Provide faithful preaching.
—The late F. L. Reed to James C. Perkins

The one who uses effectively and with integrity his gifts for ministry will have more given to him. Conversely, the one who does not use his gifts wisely will have them taken away.

—The late Negail Rudolph Riley to Cain Hope Felder

Pastors must be impeccably trained. They must strive for excellence.

—The late Benjamin E. Mays to Thomas Kilgore, Jr.

What God is doing is bigger than we are, and his message must be proclaimed. Even though the vessel that carries the message may be flawed, the message remains pure.

—The late A. Edward Davis to H. Beecher Hicks, Jr.

Pastors must minister to people in a calm and moderate way.

—The late Sandy Ray to Bennett W. Smith, Sr.

The pastor must take the time to read, study, and spend time with God. The pastor must also have a sense of humor and a sense of humility.

—The late Frank M. Reid, Jr., to Frank M. Reid III

Pastors must be caring.

—The late Matthew A. Watley to William D. Watley

Be an independent thinker. If you cannot think for yourself, then someone else will do your thinking for you. Whoever does your thinking for you will be your master, and you will be that person's slave.

—The late Benjamin E. Mays to Amos Brown

There are no great pastors; there are great people.

—The late A. J. BeBelle to Gus Roman

No matter what happens, the pastor must have a sense of hope.
—*The late M. Marquette Peace, Sr., to William B. Moore*

Preachers must have a love for the language.
—*The late William A. Jones, Sr., to William A. Jones, Jr.*

If there is no joy in the struggle and trials of ministry, try another profession.
—*The late L. G. Fields to Joseph E. Lowery*

When dealing with the church, things must be done decently and in order.
—*The late Wade Hampton McKinney to Samuel B. McKinney*

There is no substitute for hard work. God rewards your faithfulness. Whatever you do, do it well.
—*The late Ernest Moore to Joe S. Ratliff*

The preacher must build a library and be a constant reader.
—*The late T. R. Washington to Repsie Warren*

Rome was not built in one day. The pastor must plan his work and work his plan. There is power in prayer and meditation. If you can pray it through, God will show you where, when, and how to do! The pastor must balance inspiration and intellect.
—*The late Howard Thurman to T. Garrott Benjamin, Jr.*

When preachers preach, they must engage in dialogue with the passage.
—*The late J. Pius Barbour to William A. Jones, Jr.*

Whatever else I am, I am first a pastor and a preacher.
—*The late Ralph David Abernathy to J. Wendell Mapson, Jr.*

Blossom where you are. Preach and pastor as though you were in the greatest church house in the nation.
—*The late M. Marquette Peace, Sr., to M. Marquette Peace, Jr.*

Do not tamper with people's souls.
—*The late Isaac R. Clark, Sr., to Katie G. Cannon*

You can send a small person to a big church, and in no time he or she will whittle it down to his or her size. Conversely, you can send a big person to a small situation, and with the Lord's help and the people's support, he or she will build it up to fantastic proportions.
—*The late J. W. E. Bowen to Corneilius Henderson*

When it comes to interpreting Scripture, the first law of biblical interpretation is a correct reading of the passage. If you do not read it correctly, you cannot interpret it correctly.
—*The late Roy Arthur Mayfield to Caesar A. W. Clark*

The pastor must love God and love the people.
—*The late William E. Gardner, Sr., to Calvin O. Butts III*

Minister within the orbit of your gift.
—*The late J. Pius Barbour to Charles E. Booth*

Make the sermon plain.
—*The late Sandy Ray to J. Alfred Smith, Sr.*

A call to the ministry is a call to preparation.
—*The late Rufus Hill to Otis Moss, Jr.*

Whatever you do, do it so well that the living, the dead, and the unborn could not do it any better. Never allow the world to dismiss you because of lazy or sloppy work. If you are going to preach, preach so well that even those who do not like you must admit that you are a man or a person of God. . . . It is dishonest to go into the pulpit unprepared. It is as dishonest as a bank robber robbing a bank. It is as dishonest as an embezzler. But when you are prepared, always go on your knees and seek the guidance of Eternal God.

—*The late Benjamin E. Mays to Otis Moss, Jr.*

Before you go into a fight, make sure you know who your troops are. Before going into any battle in the church, know where the land mines are.

—*The late J. H. Jackson to J. Wendell Mapson, Jr.*

Believe what you say from the bottom of your heart, and preach it and teach it with all the power you can muster.

—*The late William Holmes Borders to Otis Moss, Jr.*

A great preacher is not just one who has a loud voice or one who can engage in dramatic antics but one who lives close the heartbeat of humanity and the Spirit of Jesus.

—*The late I. B. Loud to Cecil Williams*

The pastor must be involved in personal meditation and spiritual discipline. You cannot give out what you do not have. You cannot constantly continue to feed the masses if you yourself are spiritually anorectic. The preacher must learn to listen to the silence and hear God and, in the midst of pain, see the face of God.

—*The late Howard Thurman to Susan D. Newman*

One day Old Man Timberlake asked me, "Campbell, can you write a sermon?" Being at Morehouse in my first semester, I said, "Yes, I can write a sermon." Then Timberlake said, "Write *this,*" as he stroked the air with his hand. I said to him, "That is just a gesture; that's not a sermon." He said to me, "The day will come

when that will be all that you have. Your hoop will fail. Arthritis may take your swoop, and you must be able to transmit the gospel with whatever you have left."
—*The late Rev. (Old Man) Timberlake to Anthony Campbell*

Burn in the pulpit. When you burn in the pulpit, the people will come to see you burn!
—*The late Bishop Bryant to Vashti McKenzie*

The pastor must have absolute integrity. If you have no character in ministry, you have nothing.
—*The late Joseph L. Roberts, Sr., to Joseph L. Roberts, Jr.*

Exercise your duty without the appearance of being burdened.
—*The late C. C. Adams to Marshall L. Shepard, Jr.*

Wear easily the trappings of office.
—*The late Frank M. Reid, Jr., to Marshall L. Shepard, Jr.*

Maintain discipline.
—*The late Nelson H. Smith, Sr., to Nelson H. Smith, Jr.*

Don't be a lazy preacher and pastor.
—*The late William Holmes Borders to Nelson H. Smith, Jr.*

Don't be afraid to think and use the mind as a gift from God for the edifying of the people of God. Don't be afraid to walk alone. The thinker and the prophet are usually lonely figures. God will hold you up, even when you stand alone.
—*The late Robert E. Roberts to Robert M. Franklin*

Read everything.
—*The late F. Douglas Ferrell to Aidsand Wright-Riggins*

Start where the people are, and speak to them in a language and cultural idiom that they understand on your way to taking them to where they need to go.
—*The late Martin Luther King, Jr., to Jesse L. Jackson*

Wear your worries like a loose garment.
—*The late John Wesley Wiley to Dennis W. Wiley*

Ministry in the parish and ministry in education are two of the highest callings a human being can ever have.
—*The late William H. Gray, Jr., to William H. Gray III*

The power of the gospel is the most valuable resource the preacher has.
—*The late Brady Johnson to Forrest Harris*

The pastor practitioner should develop a feel for critical scholarship.
—*The late J. Pius Barbour to Wallace C. Smith*

Preachers must be spiritually grounded.
—*The late Martin Luther King, Jr., to Wallace C. Smith*

The way of Christ is not a crossless way. But if Christ is with us, and we are with him, we can survive, and we can be effective.
—*The late William Hunter Hester to G. Daniel Jones*

To build ministries requires the longevity of the pastor in a particular congregation. Be patient with the people.
—*The late Rudolph Robinson to Jesse Brown, Jr.*

When you go to a new church, you will not be the pastor; you have to become the pastor.
—*The late Sandy Ray to Albert Campbell*

The pastor must be open and receive people. The pastor also needs someone with whom to talk and to share his or her deepest pains as well as greatest joys.

—The late Alfred Morgan Waller, Jr., to H. Dean Trulear

Do not attempt to change what has been in the church. Enlighten the people with the light that you have to share, but don't blind them!

—The late Marshall Shepard, Sr., to J. Wendell Mapson, Sr.

Take the church that you have and work as hard as you can and make as much of it as you can, and you will have a large church and a good church. Take whatever the Lord gives you, lest you run the risk of being fired by God. The worst thing in the world is to be fired by God.

—The late Earl L. Harrison to L. Venchael Booth

The pastor must be fully acquainted with Scripture.

—The late George W. Massey, Sr., to James E. Massey

The preacher must be prophetic in preaching. The preacher must be audacious.

—The late Raymond S. Jackson to James E. Massey

The preacher must probe a text for its depth.

—The late Howard Thurman to James E. Massey

In this life, the African American must bite off more than he can chew, and chew it. He must set out to do more than he can do, and do it.

—The late Henry Nichols to Robert Johnson-Smith II

If you can pray a lot, you can take a lot.

—The late Rev. Barnett to Floyd Massey, Jr.

Ministry is a full-time job, and you ought to give it your best.
—*The late Harrison James Bryant to John R. Bryant*

The pastor must understand the grace of God and how it applies to the congregation.
—*The late Samuel Grimes to Arthur Brazier*

The pastor must understand the full scope of pastoral work.
—*The late E. Franklin Jackson to Cecil Bishop*

Never let your people see you lose your temper.
—*The late M. W. Newsome to Arlee Griffin, Jr.*

The preacher should be involved in social justice, grounded in the teachings of Jesus.
—*The late Vernon Johns to Wyatt Tee Walker*

If you are faithful in the discharge of your mission and ministry, somehow the Lord will take care of what the end product should be.
—*The late Martin Luther King, Jr., to Wyatt Tee Walker*

Look to Jesus as your example. . . . If God has called you to do a job, then there is no one on earth who can do it like you or prevent you from doing it.
—*The late W. H. R. Powell to Catherine I. Godboldte*

Give God your best no matter where you are. Learn to trust the people.
The late Timothy B. Echols to Evans E. Crawford

The following people shared their wisdom with the contributors of this book through living exemplary lives:

Reuben Fheares
Dewit Graham
Samuel G. Stevens
James Hall, Sr.
Benjamin F. Glasco
J. J. Abney
Charles Freeman
V. M. Bailey
J. C. Jackson
John Bailey
Washington Monroe Taylor
Moses Newton
David Jesse Jones
James H. Evans, Sr.
Ezekiel Carolina
Mother Dabney
John W. Williams
Reggie Johnson
E. A. Adams
John B. Henderson
R. H. Bolden
D. C. Rice
E. E. Smith
Edward W. Murray
E. R. Harrison
F. D. Robinson
D. A. Holmes
Steven Dynamoe Campbell
Miles Mark Fisher
Berkley L. Hall
H. H. Coleman
John M. Elerson
Bravid Harris
Samuel A. Wilson

M. C. Williams
R. W. Campbell
Perry Smith
Edward H. Freeman
Henry McNeil Turner
Gordon Blaine Hancock
Charles Andrew Hill, Sr.
Cornell E. Talley
John W. Walker, Sr.

Conclusion

It is my hope that the readers of this book will draw their own conclusions as they read, and read again, the words that are written in this work. I hope that the wisdom shared in these pages will help clergypersons of all ages to further build God's kingdom here on earth. It is also my hope that this work will spark dialogue amongst clergy across racial and denominational lines so that this wisdom can be further refined and used in the local church. I hope that clergypersons from all denominations, male and female, old and young, will come to realize that we have a lot in common and that we are all in the struggle together. Collectively, we can successfully combat the principalities and powers of our day by using our education, our resources, our history, our faith, and, of course, the wisdom that has been developed by, and passed down to, the African American preacher—the wisdom of the ages.

Annotated Bibliography

This annotated bibliography has been compiled specifically for *Wisdom of the Ages: The Mystique of the African American Preacher*. The first section contains resources on preaching (homiletics). The second section lists resources written about the African American preacher, with a focus on role and image. The third section contains biographical resources about specific African American preachers, and the fourth, resources on pastoral care in the African American church. The fifth section suggests resources that focus on church administration, including resources on the operation of the church, both internal and external (social outreach). The final section includes resources on the African American church that have been considered by many to be "classic." These "classic" resources are included to provide a total picture of the life and scope of the African American preacher.

Resources on Preaching (Homiletics)

Preaching is at the core of the being of the African American preacher. The late Sandy Ray shared wisdom with Manuel Scott, Sr., by saying that, "The one thing that the preacher can do that no one else in the church can do is preach." Preaching cannot be delegated to a layperson or an officer; it must be done by a preacher.

There have been numerous books written that contain collections of sermons by noted African American preachers. While these resources are not included in this bibliography, they serve as valuable examples of the uniqueness of the preaching styles of African American preachers. The focus of this section of the bibliography is not so much on the finished product but on the process in which the sermon is developed—the preparation of the sermon. In the area of homiletics in the African American church, there are two major writers: James Earl Massey and Henry H. Mitchell. Both have done extensive work in the area of preaching.

Massey, the associate professor of homiletics and worship at Anderson College's Graduate School of Theology, takes a very straightforward, practical approach to preaching and offers concrete methods for sermon preparation and preaching. A writer of thirteen books on preaching, he has probably written more on preaching than any other African American preacher. One his most noted works is *Designing the Sermon*.

Mitchell, currently a visiting professor at the Interdenominational Theological Center, has written the classic works in *Black Preaching* and *The Recovery of Preaching*. While he offers concrete methods for sermon preparation and preaching, Mitchell has a strong historical focus in his works. His methods stem from the cultural experience of African American people and have a heavy emphasis on celebration.

Other noted works on preaching include Warren Stewart's *Interpreting God's Word in Black Preaching*, Samuel Proctor's *"How Shall They Hear?"* and Gardner Taylor's *How Shall They Preach?*

Boulware, Marcus. *The Oratory of Negro Leaders Nineteen Hundred–Nineteen Sixty-Eight.* Westport, Conn.: Negro Universities Press, 1969 A fine analysis of oratory styles of various African American leaders. Chapter eight focuses on the oratory styles of women, including Nannie Helen Boroughs, Charlotte Hawkins Brown, and Mary McLeod Bethune.

Ellison, John Malcus. *They Who Preach.* Nashville: Broadman Press, 1956. Discusses the role of the preacher and the congregation during the preaching experience, how to build a sermon, how to choose a theme, and the use of illustrations in the sermon.

Forbes, James. *The Holy Spirit and Preaching.* Nashville: Abingdon Press, 1989. The first African American pastor of the Riverside Church, Forbes discusses the role of the Holy Spirit in preaching, sermon preparation, and the spiritual formation of anointed preachers. These lectures were originally delivered at the Lyman Beecher Lectures. His philosophy reflects his origins in the United Holy Church of America.

Goodwin, Bennie E. *The Effective Preacher.* Atlanta: Goodpatrick Publishers, 1987.

Hicks, H. Beecher, Jr. "Bones, Sinew, Flesh and Blood Coming to Life." In *Inside the Sermon: Thirteen Preachers Discuss Their Methods of Preparing Messages.* Edited by Richard Allen Bodey, 111-123. Grand Rapids: Baker Book House, 1990. Hicks gives a step-by-step description on his method of sermon preparation. He uses Ezekiel's "dry bones" scenario to make his point.

King, D. E. *Preaching to Preachers.* Warminster, Pa.: Neibauer Press. 1984.

Massey, James Earl. *The Responsible Pulpit.* Anderson, Ind.: Warner Press, 1974.

_____. *The Sermon in Perspective: A Study of Communications and Charisma.* Grand Rapids: Baker Book House, 1976. Massey discusses the sermon in perspective from five angles: communication, counsel, creation, charisma, and commentary.

_____. *Designing the Sermon: Order and Movement in Preaching.* Edited by William D. Thompson. Nashville: Abingdon Press, 1980. James Massey focuses on the goal or outcome of the sermon and how the preacher is going to reach the goal. He discusses the narrative sermon, the expository sermon, and the topical sermon. He also includes a section on the development of the funeral sermon.

Mitchell, Henry H. *Black Preaching.* San Francisco: Harper and Row, 1978. After giving an historical background of black preaching, Mitchell discusses the style, content, and techniques of black preaching. He also discusses the use of black English, delivery, and the role of celebration in the sermon.

_____. *The Recovery of Preaching.* San Francisco: Harper and Row, 1977. Mitchell stresses that the preacher must have a thorough knowledge of the Bible and must know how to apply this knowledge to the life experiences of the listeners. The preacher must learn to sit where the listener sits.

_____. *Celebration and Experience in Preaching.* Nashville: Abingdon Press, 1990. In this book Mitchell discusses how to use imagination, emotive expression, and celebration to meet the emotional and rational needs of people. He demonstrates how to use celebration within literary genres such as biblical narratives and character sketches. Examples of sermons are also included.

Morris, Calvin. "Martin Luther King: Exemplary Preacher." *Journal of the Interdenominational Theological Center,* 4, no. 2 (Spring 1977). Morris discusses the preaching style of Martin Luther King, Jr. He contends that the elements of exemplary preaching are: (1) The sermon must speak out of and to the faith of both the speaker and the hearer; (2) The preaching and the preacher must be one, and the sermon must have an unmistakable cosmic note, a sense of community; (3) The sermon must proclaim the cross; and (4) The sermon must meet the needs of people. The article also contains an excellent bibliography of works about Martin Luther King, Jr.

Moyd, Olin P. *The Sacred Art.* Valley Forge: Judson Press, 1995. Moyd shows that through preaching, practical theology has been conveyed to the congregation. He uses illustrations from noted African American preachers to make his point.

_____ "Elements of Black Preaching." *The Journal of Religious Thought,* XXX, no. 1 (1973): 58. Olin Moyd discusses the style and design of the preaching of Sandy Ray. He concludes that there are five characteristics of his preaching: telling the Bible story; repetition, rhythm, and rest; testimony; liberation; and celebration.

Neubald, Robert T. *Black Preaching.* Philadelphia: The Geneva Press, 1977.

Pipes, William H. *Say Amen, Brother, Old-Time Negro Preaching: A Study in American Frustration.* 1951. Reprint. Westport, Conn.: Negro Universities Press, 1970. Discusses black preaching in the South and contends that a mixture of African and American heritage are combined to create this style of preaching. A collection of sermons is included. Discusses the logical argument of black preaching, modes of persuasion, emotional appeal, delivery, and style of black preaching.

Proctor, Samuel D. *The Certain Sound of the Trumpet: Crafting a Sermon of Authority.* Valley Forge: Judson Press, 1994. Samuel Proctor gives a step-by-step method for sermon development.

_____. *"How Shall They Hear?" Effective Preaching for Vital Faith.* Valley Forge: Judson Press, 1992. Proctor promotes four vital faith issues: the celebration of God's presence and participation in human affairs, the assurance of spiritual renewal and moral wholeness, the affirmation of a hope for a genuine human community, and the awareness of the eternal in the midst of time.

Rosenberg, Bruce A. *The Art of the American Folk Preacher.* New York: Oxford University Press, 1970. Rosenberg gives a detailed description of the development of the sermon. He studies the preaching styles of preachers from various parts of the country.

Smith, J. Alfred, Sr. *Preach On!* Nashville: Broadman Press, 1984. Smith discusses various styles of preaching, the study of words and poetic diction, figures of speech, and the use of the voice. Sermons from some of his students are also included. There is also an interesting section on the oratory and style of modern black preachers.

Spillers, Hortense J. "Martin Luther King and the Style of the Black Sermon." *Black Scholars* (September 1977).

Stewart, Warren H. Sr. *Interpreting God's Word in Black Preaching.* Valley Forge: Judson Press, 1984.

Stewart offers a well-defined five-point study on the hermeneutical process. Each principle is illustrated through excerpts from the sermons of Sandy F. Ray; William A. Jones, Jr.; and Manuel L. Scott, Sr.

Taylor, Gardner C. *How Shall They Preach?* Elgin, Ill.: Progressive Baptist Publishing House, 1977. A written account of the Lyman Beecher Lectures, 1975–1976. The book contains Taylor's analysis of sermon preparation and a discussion of the foolishness of preaching. His sermons are also included.

Tinney, James S. "The 'Miracle' of Black Preaching." *Christianity Today,* 20, no. 9 (30 January 1976): 14-16. Tinney presents six elements that constitute black preaching and make it unique:

antiphonal call and response; pacing, cadence, and rhythm; sentence forms; formulas; melody; dramatics.

Trulear, H. Dean. "The Lord Will Make a Way Somehow: Black Worship in the Afro-American Story." *Journal of the Interdenominational Theological Center,* 13, no. 1 (Fall 1985): 87-104. In his discussion of worship in the black church, Trulear comments on the preaching styles of African American preachers. An analysis of the preaching style of William Augustus Jones, pastor of the Bethany Baptist Church in Brooklyn, New York, is included.

Warren, Mervyn A. "A Rhetorical Study of the Preaching of Doctor Martin Luther King, Jr., Pastor and Pulpit Orator" Ph.D. diss., Michigan State University, 1966.

Resources on the African American Preacher

The African American preacher has been a unique figure throughout history. The African American preacher has had to wear many hats and work in many arenas. While dealing with demands that preachers and pastors of all races have had to deal with, the African American preacher has had the added burden of combating the evil of racism in this country, as well as its derivatives, such as poverty, poor housing, and unequal school systems, to name a few. How was the preacher able to handle these demands and still keep the faith?

A number of writers have written about the African American preacher and what makes him or her tick. The resources in this section touch on the makeup of the African American preacher. This section is the shortest of all the sections. There is a need for more research in this area. Perhaps *Wisdom of the Ages* will help fill this void.

The most noted work in this area is Charles V. Hamilton's *The Black Preacher in America.* While it was written in 1972, it contains discussions on issues that are still relevant to today's preacher. Other noted works include H. Beecher Hicks, Jr.'s *Images of the Black Preacher* and Joseph Johnson's *The Soul of the Black Preacher.*

Adams, John H. *The Black Pulpit Revolution in the United Methodist Church and Other Denominations.* Chicago: Strugglers'

odist Church and Other Denominations. Chicago: Strugglers'
Community Press, 1985. Discusses the challenges, problems,
and achievements of the African American Methodist preacher.
Based on the life struggles and toils of an African American
Methodist preacher.

Childs, John Brown. *The Political Black Minister: A Study in
African American Politics and Religion*. Boston: G. K. Hall and
Co., 1980. Childs looks at the connection between black religion
and political action. He focuses on three pastors and their involvement in political action. A good treatise on the dilemma
faced by African American preachers in the area of political
involvement.

Daniel, W. A. *The Education of Negro Ministers*. New York: George
H. Doran, 1925.

Fauset, Arthur H. *Black Gods of the Metropolis: Negro Religious
Cults of the Urban North*. Philadelphia: University of Pennsyl-
vania Press, 1971. Discusses the rise of various religious groups
and cults that made a significant impact on the lives of African
American people. Included are profiles on Father Divine and
Bishop Grace.

Foley, Albert S. *God's Men of Color: The Colored Catholic Priests
of the United States 1854–1954*. New York: Farrar Strauss, 1955.

Hamilton, Charles V. *The Black Preacher in America*. New York:
William Morrow and Co., 1972. A socio-political study of the
African American preacher that discusses history, development,
emerging problems, education, and political activism. While
Hamilton presents a tentative description of the African Ameri-
can preacher, he concludes by saying that there is no "typical"
African American preacher.

Harris, James H. *Black Ministers and Laity in the Urban Church:
An Analysis of Political and Social Expectations*. Lanham, Md.:
University Press of America, 1987.

Hicks, H. Beecher, Jr. *Images of the Black Preacher*. Valley Forge:
Judson Press, 1977. Discusses the slave preacher and offers
contemporary images of the black preacher, both positive and
negative. Offers new perspectives for the black preacher.

Hong, Lawrence K., and Marion V. Daerman. "The Street Corner

Preacher: Sowing Good Seeds by the Wayside." *Urban Life*, 67, no. 1 (April 1977): 56-67. The writers contend that while the street-corner preacher may appear to be disarrayed and frenzied, he is in reality a rational, dedicated Christian with a complex organization of his own. The writers note that many street-corner preachers are doing a fine work, while many in the organized church consider them to be an embarrassment.

Johnson, Joseph. *The Soul of the Black Preacher*. Philadelphia: Pilgrim Press, 1971. A collection of sermons and lectures by the author. The focus is on Jesus as the liberator of the oppressed and the preacher's role in this liberation. Discusses the motivations and struggles of the African American preacher, the gifts of the preacher, and the heritage of the preacher.

Richardson, Marilyn. *Black Women in Religion: A Bibliography*. Boston: G. K. Hall & Co., 1980. A bibliography of works by and about African American women in religion. Annotated.

Shockley, Grant, et al. *Black Pastors in United Methodism*. Atlanta: Center for Research and Social Change, Emory University, 1976. Discusses pastors as leaders and black church development. Contains demographics about the United Methodist church.

Welty, William M. "Black Shepherds: A Study of the Leading Negro Clergymen in New York City 1900–1940." Ph.D. diss., New York University, 1969. Discusses the leading clergy in New York City during these years. Done in a chronological order to reflect the different eras in Harlem.

Wright, Richard R., Jr. *The Bishops of the African Methodist Episcopal Church*. Nashville: A.M.E. Sunday School Union, 1963.

Biography

This section contains works about specific African American preachers, pastors, and scholars. I hope that a study of the lives of great pastors and preachers will help pastors of today and in years to come gain knowledge and wisdom from the experiences of others. While this section of the bibliography is lengthy, it only scratches the surface. I have focused on the representative works that discuss the formation of the thought of the person in the biography. It is not the attempt of this bibliography to include works that discuss the actual thought of these persons. In most cases, the autobiography of the individual preacher is included as opposed to what someone else may have written about that person.

It is quite clear that the preacher with the most resources written about him is Martin Luther King, Jr. I've included only a few of the most noted works about him in this bibliography. For a detailed bibliography on King, see *Martin Luther King, Jr.: A Comprehensive Bibliography* from the King Library Archives. Adam Clayton Powell, Jr., is another preacher who has had a number of works written about him.

Allen, Richard. *The Life Experience and Gospel Labors of the Rt. Rev. Richard Allen.* 2d ed. Nashville: Abingdon Press, 1960. An account of the rise of the African Methodist Episcopal church and the development of Allen's thought. Written by Allen, with an introduction by George A. Singleton.

Baldwin, Lewis V. *There Is a Balm in Gilead: The Cultural Roots of Martin Luther King, Jr.* Minneapolis: Augsburg Fortress Press, 1991. Baldwin argues that King's African American Christian tradition had a significant impact on his thinking and his appropriation of Gandhi's thought, as well as many of the Western philosophers and theologians.

Bennett, Lerone, Jr. *What Manner of Man: A Biography of Martin Luther King, Jr.* Chicago: Johnson Publishing Co., 1964. Bennett gives a detailed description of the life of Martin Luther King, Jr. The book discusses the influence of his parents, Morehouse College, and Dr. Benjamin Elijah Mays on the formation of his thought. The book contains an introduction by Mays.

Boddie, Charles Emerson. *God's Bad Boys.* Valley Forge: Judson Press, 1972. Biographical information on eight preachers: Russell Conwell Barbour; J. Timothy Boddie; E. C. Estell; Vernon Johns; Jesse Jai McNeil; Marshall L. Shepard, Sr.; Martin Luther King, Jr.; and James Edward Rose.

Burnham, Kenneth E. *God Comes to America: Father Divine and the Peace Mission Movement.* New York: Lambeth Press, 1978.

Cadbury, M. *The Life of Amanda Smith: The African Sybil, The*

Christian Saint. Birmingham: Cornish Brothers, 1960. The story of Amanda Smith, who made her reputation as an inspiring singer at revivals and went on to become an internationally known missionary and evangelist. She preached in India, Africa, and throughout the United States.

Cone, James H. *My Soul Looks Back*. Nashville: Abingdon Press, 1982. Contains Cone's autobiographical history of the development of his theology. He discusses the influence of feminism, Marxism, and third-world theologies, as well as his formal education.

Cone, James H. *Martin & Malcom & America: A Dream or a Nightmare*. Maryknoll: Orbis Books, 1991. While Cone discusses the different philosophies of Martin Luther King, Jr., and Malcom X, he also presents biographical information to give a basis for the development of their thought.

Du Bois, W. E. B. *The Autobiography of W. E. B. Du Bois: A Soliloquy on Viewing My Life from the Last Decade of Its First Century*. New York: International Publishers Company, Inc., 1968. An account of the life of Du Bois, beginning in his childhood and going through his entire life and education, works and travels.

English, James W. *Handyman of the Lord: The Life and Ministry of Rev. William Holmes Borders*. New York: Meredith Press, 1967. The story of Border's struggle out of poverty, his quest for education, and his efforts to meet the needs of his people. The book also discusses his pastorate at the Wheat Street Baptist Church in Atlanta, Georgia.

Felton, Ralph A. *Go Down Moses: A Study of Twenty One Successful Negro Rural Pastors*. Madison, N.J.: Department of the Rural Church, Drew Theological Seminary, 1952. Discusses the lives of twenty-one rural pastors who have done outstanding jobs with their churches. This study emerged out of a conference at Gammon Theological Seminary in Atlanta, Georgia.

Foner, Phillip S., ed. *Black Socialist Preacher*. San Francisco: Synthesis Publications, 1983. The story of George Washington Woodbey, a national leader of African American socialists in the early twentieth century. A collection of Woodbey's works that urge African Americans to adopt socialism. The book also contains works by his disciple, George W. Slater.

Franklin, Robert Michael. *Liberating Visions: Human Fulfillment and Social Justice in African American Thought.* Minneapolis: Augsburg Fortress Press, 1990. An analysis of the thought of Booker T. Washington, W. E. B. Du Bois, Malcom X, and Martin Luther King, Jr. Franklin includes a biographical sketch of each thinker to provide a background for their thinking.

Gray, Thomas. *The Confessions of Nat Turner, the Leader of the Late Insurrection in Southhampton, Virginia.* Baltimore: Lucas and Deaver, 1831.

Harlan, Howard H. *John Jasper—A Case History in Leadership.* Charlottesville, Va.: University of Virginia Press, 1936.

Haskins, James. *Adam Clayton Powell: Portrait of a Marching Black.* New York: Dial Press, 1974.

Hatcher, William E. *John Jasper, The Unmatched Negro Philosopher and Preacher.* New York: Revell, 1908. An account of the life of Jasper, a noted slave preacher who founded the Sixth Mt. Zion Baptist Church in Richmond, Virginia. He gained national fame from his sermon "The Sun Do Move," where he argued from a biblical perspective that the sun rotates around the earth.

Hoshor, John. *God in a Rolls Royce: The Rise of Father Divine.* New York: Hillman-Curl, 1936. Early biography of Father Divine (George Baker).

Jackson, Jesse L. *Straight from the Heart.* Edited by Roger Hatchard and Frank E. Watkins. Philadelphia: Fortress Press, 1987. His own statement. A comprehensive collection that includes his thoughts and ideas on human rights, politics, education, and peace.

Jenness, Mary. "A City Pastor, William Loyd Imes." In *Twelve Negro Americans.* New York: Friendship Press, 1936. A biographical sketch of an urban pastor.

Johnson, Suzan D. *Wise Women Bearing Gifts.* Valley Forge: Judson Press, 1988. Portraits of courageous women who dared to answer God's call despite the overwhelming barriers they faced in a traditionally "men only" world. The forward is by Ella Mitchell.

Jones, Ralph H. *Charles Albert Tindley: Prince of Preachers.* Nashville: Abingdon Press, 1982. The life of the master preacher, orator, and leader. The son of a former slave, with no formal education, he would go on to read Greek and Hebrew and write forty hymns.

King, Martin Luther, Jr. *Stride Toward Freedom: The Montgomery Story.* New York: Harper, 1958. The story of the Montgomery bus boycott. Also gives biographical information that focuses on the formation of King's nonviolent stance.

King, Martin Luther, Sr. *Daddy King: An Autobiography, with Clayton Riley.* New York: William Morrow, 1980. A depiction of the entire King family. The focus is on Martin Luther King, Sr., the son of a sharecropper, and his work at the Ebenezer Baptist Church in Atlanta, Georgia. The book discusses "Daddy" King's struggles with voter registration, equal pay for teachers, and other civil injustices.

Lee, Jarena. "Following the Trails of the Fathers: The First Female Preacher." *A.M.E. Church Review* (October–December 1964). A brief discussion of the life and works of Jarena Lee, the first woman licensed to preach in the African Methodist Episcopal Church. A portrait of her in 1844 at age sixty.

Licorish, Joshua. *Harry Hoosier: African Pioneer Preacher.* Philadelphia: Afro-Methodist Press, 1967. The story of the man known as "Black Harry," born near Fayetteville, North Carolina. His rise as a local preacher, one who became one of the most eloquent preachers of his day in the Methodist church.

Lischer, Richard. *The Preacher King.* New York: Oxford University Press, 1995. Lischer investigates Martin Luther King, Jr.'s religious development, from the early years as a "preacher's kid" to his prophetic rage that condemned American and religious hypocrisy in the final years of his life.

Lovett, Bobby L. *A Black Man's Dream, The First One Hundred Years: The Story of R. H. Boyd.* The Mega Corporation, 1993.

Martin Luther King, Jr.: A Comprehensive Bibliography. Atlanta: The King Library Archives, 1985.

Mays, Benjamin E. *Born to Rebel: An Autobiography by Benjamin E. Mays.* Athens, Ga.: University of Georgia Publishers, 1986.

The autobiography of a man raised in poverty who would go on to earn a Ph.D. from University of Chicago. Mays, who was president of Morehouse College for twenty-seven years, helped shape the lives of a generation of African American men, including Martin Luther King, Jr.

McClain, William B. *Black People in the United Methodist Church: Whither Thou Goest?* Nashville: Abingdon Press, 1984. Contains accounts of the lives of Harry Hoosier, Henry Evans, and John Stewart.

Norton, Will. "John Perkins: The Stature of a Servant." *Christianity Today*, 24, no. 1 (January 1, 1982): 18-27.

Oates, Stephen B. *Let the Trumpet Sound: The Life of Martin Luther King, Jr.* New York: Harper and Row, 1985. Stories of King's life, collected and retold.

Perkins, John. *Let Justice Roll Down: John Perkins Tells His Own Story.* Glendale, Calif.: Regal Books, 1976. The founder of Calvary Ministries gives an account of his life. He discusses his three-fold approach to ministry: biblical evangelism, Christian education, and social action and community development.

Powell, Adam Clayton, Jr. *Adam on Adam: The Autobiography of Adam Clayton Powell.* New York: Dial, 1971. 1994 Reprint. New York: Carol Publishing Group, 1994.

Powell, Adam Clayton, Sr. *Against the Tide. An Autobiography.* New York: R. R. Smith, 1938.

Smith, Amanda Berry. *An Autobiography: The Story of the Lord's Dealings with Mrs. Amanda Smith, the Colored Evangelist.* Chicago: Meyer and Brother, 1893; New York: Oxford University Press, 1988. Contains an account of her life, her call to ministry, and her preaching throughout the world. She was noted for being an independent missionary and drawing large crowds when she preached.

Smith, Famous. *A Man Called Famous: Elder Famous Smith.* Edited by Ida Sykes. West Memphis, Ark.: Fifteenth Street Church of God in Christ, 1983.

Smith, Warren Thomas. *Harry Hoosier: Circuit Rider.* Nashville: The Upper Room, United Methodist Church, 1981.

Thurman, Howard. *With Head and Heart: The Autobiography of*

Howard Thurman. New York: Harcourt Brace Jovanovich, 1979. An autobiography that discusses Thurman's development, beginning at Morehouse College and Rochester Theological Seminary, and his career at Oberlin College and Howard University. It also portrays his pilgrimage to India and Africa and discusses his writings.

Trotman, C. James. "Matthew Anderson: Black Pastor, Churchman, and Social Reformer." *American Presbyterian*, 66, no. 1 (Spring 1988): 11-21. The story of the founder and pastor of the Berean Presbyterian Church in Philadelphia, Pennsylvania. This pioneer went on to start a vocational school and a bank. Anderson was the prototype of the twentieth-century urban pastor.

Watley, William D. *Roots of Resistance: The Nonviolent Ethic of Martin Luther King, Jr.* Valley Forge: Judson Press, 1985. Watley discusses the formative influences of King, his religious experience, and the six principles of his nonviolent ethic. Also contains an excellent bibliography of works done by and about King.

Webb, Lillian A. *About My Father's Business: The Life of Elder Michaux.* Westport, Conn.: Greenwood Press, 1981.

Williams, Cecil. *I Am Alive: An Autobiography.* San Francisco: Harper and Row, 1988. At the time of the writing, Williams was the innovative and controversial pastor of the Glide Memorial United Methodist Church in San Francisco.

Williams, Ethel L. *Biographical Directory of Negro Ministers.* 3d ed. Boston: G. K. Hall & Co., 1975. Gives biographical information on pastors and preachers in the United States. Includes pastorates, education, and writings.

Young, Henry. *Major Black Religious Leaders 1755–1940.* Nashville: Abingdon Press, 1977. An examination of the lives of twelve religious leaders. The book includes major urban figures such as Richard Allen, David Walker, Nat Turner, and Marcus Garvey. Discusses the theologies and contributions of each.

_____. *Major Black Religious Leaders Since 1940.* Nashville: Abingdon Press, 1979. The book includes the theologies and contributions of leaders such as Martin Luther King, Jr.; James Cone; Jesse Jackson; and Benjamin Mays.

Pastoral Care

There are a number of good resources relating to pastoral care in the African American church. Most of the resources contend that pastoral care must be done in the context of the African American community. The author who has done the most extensive work in this area is Edward P. Wimberly, associate professor of pastoral theology at Garrett-Evangelical Theological Seminary. Wimberly's work is both biblical and cultural. He writes in a comprehensive style and touches on the pertinent areas of African American life. One of his most noted works is *Pastoral Care in the Black Church.* Other noted works include Clarence Walker's *Biblical Counseling with African Americans* and Benjamin Baker's *Shepherding the Sheep.*

Baker, Benjamin S. *Shepherding the Sheep.* Nashville: Broadman Press, 1983. An in-depth manual that discusses the pastor as pastor, pastor as preacher; pastor as teacher; pastor as healer; pastor as priest; pastor as prophet-servant.

Birchett, Colleen. *How to Help Hurting People.* Chicago: Urban Ministries, 1990.

Felton, Carroll M., Jr. *The Care of Souls in the Black Church.* New York: Martin Luther King Fellows Press, 1980. The focus of this book is to show that the black church has cared for and continues to care for the souls of black people. This care evolves around the soul, body, and mind. All three are interdependent. Felton contends that black people must understand themselves and the situations that they are in and do something about it rather than have others do it for them.

Gilkes, Cheryl Townsend. "The Black Church as a Therapeutic Community: Suggested Areas for Research into the Black Religious Experience." *Journal of the Interdenominational Theological Center*, 8: 29-44. Gilkes proposes that the black church has a unique therapeutic contribution to make to the community. She bases this on the argument that the black church performs four therapeutic functions: (1) The church can articulate suffering, (2) The church can locate persecutors, (3) The church provides an asylum for people to act out and validate their experiences, (4) The church fosters self-esteem.

Green, Gary. "The Black Church and the Criminal Justice System: A Pilot Project Designed to Train Black Clergy and Laymen in Pastoral Care and Counseling." D.Min. thesis, Lutheran Theological Southern Seminary, 1982.

Grey-Little, Bernadette. "Marital Quality and Power Processes Among Black Couples." *Journal of Marriage and the Family* (August 1982): 663-69.

Hurst, David. "The Shepherding of Black Christians." Th.D. diss., School of Theology at Claremont, 1981.

Jackson, Maurice. "The Black Experience with Death: A Brief Analysis Through Black Writings." *Omega* (August 1972): 204. Jackson contends that the way people handle death is strongly influenced by group membership. He argues that blacks do not take an otherworldly view of life and death. He believes that the black norm of death is secular and practical and seems to be connected to the individual's social status and interpretation of his or her most powerful experiences.

Kearney, John Henry. "The Development of a Lay Ministry of Visitation to the Hospitalized and Shut-in Members of the Mt. Calvary Missionary Baptist Church." Drew University, 1982. *Dissertation Abstracts International* vol. 43/09-A, 2950, order no. AAD83-1247.

Lattimore, Vergel L., III. "The Positive Contribution of Black Values to Pastoral Counseling." *Journal of Pastoral Care*, 34 (June 1982): 105-117. Lattimore contends that pastoral counseling requires cultural adaptations at several crucial points: collective identity, family life, work orientation. He argues that pastoral care must take place in the context of the individual's culture and community.

_____ "Pastoral Care Strategies of Black Pastors." Ph.D. diss., Northwestern University, 1984.

McAdoo, Harriet Pipes, ed. *Black Families*. Beverly Hills: Sage Publications, 1981. Contains essays by educators such as Niara Sudarkasa. Contains demographics and discusses the socialization of black families.

Parker, Matthew, and Lee N. June, comps. *The Black Family: Past, Present, and Future.* Grand Rapids: Zondervan Publishing House, 1991. A collection of sixteen essays from noted African American Christian leaders. Topics include single female parenting, teenagers, male-female relationships, the home, the role of the church, and counseling with African Americans.

Rogers, Augustus, and Edward D. Haynes. "Development of a Counseling and Referral Service in the Black Church." *Psychiatric Forum,* 12, no. 2 (Spring 1984): 48-52.

Smith, Archie, Jr. *The Relational Self: Ethics and Therapy from a Black Church Perspective.* Nashville: Abingdon Press, 1982.

Smith, Wallace Charles. *The Church in the Life of the Black Family.* Valley Forge: Judson Press, 1985.

Walker, Clarence. *Biblical Counseling with African-Americans: Taking a Ride in the Ethiopian's Chariot.* Grand Rapids: Zondervan, 1992. A practical and biblical guide that discusses ethnicity, gender, sexuality, power, socio-economics, environment, and religion. Walker then promotes a therapeutic process that includes directive engaging, affective joining, positive terminating, and cooperative involving. He also presents five biblical approaches for treatment.

Wimberly, Edward P. *Pastoral Care in the Black Church.* Nashville: Abingdon Press, 1979. One of the earliest works on pastoral care in the African American church. Wimberly discusses the issues of illness, aging, and premarital counseling, as well as the role of preaching in pastoral care.

_____. *Pastoral Counseling and Spiritual Values: A Black Point of View.* Nashville: Abingdon Press, 1982. In this book, Wimberly defines the meaning of pastoral counseling and a wholistic understanding of the human growth process. He examines the state of spirituality in pastoral counseling and its relevance to the black community.

_____. *Prayer in Pastoral Counseling.* Louisville: Westminster John Knox Press, 1990.

_____ *African-American Pastoral Care.* Nashville: Abingdon Press, 1991. In this book, Wimberly presents a narrative methodology for pastoral care. By linking personal stories and the

pastor's stories to the heart language of the Bible stories, coun-
selors can use God's unfolding drama to bring healing and
reconciliation to human lives.
Wyatt, Lawrence Paul. "Developing a Premarital Guidance Program Within a Group of Black Local Churches of God in the
Detroit, Michigan, Area." *Drew University Dissertation Abstracts International*, vol. 43/10-A, 3280.

Church Administration

While church administration is an important part of church life,
for most pastors it is the part they like the least. It is ironic that
seminaries today send ministers into the world of the pastorate
without any training in church administration. While the church
may be a spiritual haven, it is also a business. Pastors must either
attain the skills needed for the business aspects of the church or
make use of people who have these skills.

It should be noted that because of the community outreach
emphasis of the African American church, certain aspects of church
administration take place outside of the church doors. Resources in
this section include titles that discuss the issues that take place
within the church as well as those that take place outside of the
church, such as social programs.

The classic book in the area of church administration is *Church
Administration in the Black Perspective* by Floyd Massey and
Samuel McKinney. This book has been a religious bestseller for
over ten years. J. Alfred Smith, Sr., has also done a great deal of
work in this area. His works are practical and based on actual
experiences. Two of his books, *The Informed and Growing Trustee*
and *Deacons Upholding the Pastor's Arms*, are both outstanding
resources for the local church.

Anderson, Talmage. "Economic Dimensions of the Black Church:
Managerial and Financial Strategies for Survival." *Journal of the
Interdenominational Theological Center*, 13, no. 1 (1985): 39-
54. Anderson offers an economic foundation and social mission
of the black church. He discusses the religious, business, and
economic potential of the black church; innovative approaches

to giving in the black church, including deferred giving; and cost
control in the church.

Bennett, G. Willis. *Effective Urban Church Ministry.* Nashville:
Broadman Press, 1983. Based on a case study of the Allen
Temple Baptist Church in Oakland, California, where Dr. J.
Alfred Smith is pastor. Bennett discusses how to establish con-
gregational identity, plan for church growth, and celebrate
through worship.

Dillingham, Manuel Lamont. "The Role of the Pastor in Planning
and Implementing a Program of Total Ministry for a Predomi-
nately Black Baptist Congregation." D.Min. thesis, Pittsburgh
Theological Seminary, 1985.

Foster, Charles R., and Grant S. Shockley, eds. *Working with Black
Youth.* Nashville: Abingdon Press, 1989. Discusses the issues
that affect black youth living as a minority in both society and
the church. Provides a theological framework for building an
effective youth ministry that is hope-filled, evangelical, and
liberating.

Freedman, Samuel G. *Upon This Rock: The Miracles of a Black
Church.* New York: Harper Collins, 1993. Lessons in church
administration from a narrative account of the ministry of
Johnny Ray Youngblood and St. Paul's Community Baptist
Church in New York City. Exciting reading about a controversial
and innovative preacher.

Goodwin, Bennie E. *The Effective Black Church.* Atlanta: Goodpatrick Publishers, 1990.

———. *The Effective Leader.* Atlanta: Goodpatrick Publishers,
1981.

Harris, James Henry. "Laity Expectations of Ministers in the Black
Church: A Study of Political and Social Expectations in the
Context of Ministry to Community and World." Old Dominion
University, 1985. *Dissertation Abstracts International,* vol.
46/06-A, 1733.

Henderson, Perry. *The Black Church Credit Union.* Lima: Fairway
Press, 1990.

Jones, Clifford A., Sr., ed. *From Proclamation to Practice.* Valley
Forge: Judson Press, 1993. A unique work divided into two parts,

"Proclamation" and "Practice." The first section offers stewardship sermons from various African American preachers. The
second section offers the "how-tos" of stewardship. The book
includes examples of actual stewardship programs and ideas. A
very practical work.

Newman, Susan D. *With Heart and Hand: The Black Church
Working to Save Black Children.* Valley Forge: Judson Press,
1995. A practical book for starting and operating a ministry for
children. Based on the studies of ten successful model ministries.

Massey, Floyd, Jr., and Samuel McKinney. *Church Administration
in the Black Perspective.* Valley Forge: Judson Press, 1976.

Ratliff, Joe S. *Church Planting in the African-American Community.* Nashville: Broadman Press, 1993. Ratliff and Cox present
a methodology for church planting in the African American
community. The Brentwood Baptist Church, where Ratliff is
pastor, has planted eight churches in the Houston area. The
authors discuss the role of the sponsoring church and the church
planter, as well as some obstacles to church planting.

Reed, Gregory J. *Economic Empowerment Through the Church: A
Blueprint for Progressive Community Development.* Grand Rapids: Zondervan Publishing House, 1994. A practical guide that
promotes the message that the church can be very creative in the
area of economic development. Reed discusses tax strategies,
housing, day-care centers, and much more. The book also includes sample documents and forms needed for these projects.

Robinson, James J. "Bridwell Church: A Model for Ministry to
Street People in the Black Community." Ph.D. thesis, Colgate-
Rochester Divinity School, 1975.

Smith, Bennett W., Sr. *Revised Handbook on Tithing as Taught by
the Holy Scriptures.* Elgin, Ill.: Progressive Baptist Publishing
House, 1987.

Smith, J. Alfred, Sr. *The Informed and Growing Trustee.* Elgin, Ill.:
Progressive Baptist Publishing House, 1984. Smith discusses
how trustee boards should be organized and gives examples of
resources needed for day-to-day, Sunday-to-Sunday operations.
He also shares insights from eight large church trustee boards

from around the country. He concludes by discussing the role of the pastor with the trustee board.

_____. *Giving to a Giving God*. Elgin, Ill.: Progressive Baptist Publishing House, 1992. Smith begins this book with biblical lessons on giving. He then discusses the church, money, and missions. A fine set of appendices is included, with many practical tools for stewardship.

_____. *The Church in Bold Mission: A Guidebook on Black Church Development*. Atlanta: Debarment of Cooperative Ministries with National Baptists, Home Mission Board, Southern Baptist Convention, 1977.

_____. *Deacons Upholding the Pastor's Arms*. Elgin, Ill.: Progressive National Baptist Publishing House, 1983. A practical guide for the development of a solid, functional deacon board. Smith provides all of the tools needed to prepare deacons for ordination and effective ministry.

_____ "The Black Church in Economic Development." An unpublished paper read at Southern Methodist University, Dallas, 1982.

Smith, Sidney. *Ten Super Sunday Schools in the Black Community*. Nashville: Broadman Press, 1986. Case studies of ten rapidly growing Sunday schools in black churches from around the country. Includes studies of the churches of E. V. Hill, E. W. McCall, and Harold Carter.

Stallings, James O. *Telling the Story: Evangelism in Black Churches*. Valley Forge: Judson Press, 1988. Stallings contends that the most effective method of evangelism for the black church stems from the oral tradition of "telling the story." He gives an analysis of "the story" for both the storyteller and the story listener.

Stewart, Carlyle Fielding, III. *African American Church Growth: 12 Principles of Prophetic Ministry*. Nashville: Abingdon Press, 1994. Stewart defines a prophetic ministry as a means for the liberation of the church. Going beyond a simple call for social justice, he addresses the spiritual and social tyrannies, within and without the church, that preclude church growth.

Sullivan, Leon. *Build, Brother, Build*. Philadelphia: Macrae Smith

Co., 1969. The account of the formation of the Opportunities Industrialization Center, led by Sullivan. This economic development program had its roots in the African American church.

Walker, Wyatt Tee. *Common Thieves: A Tithing Manual for Black Christians and Others.* Hampton University Lectures. New York: Martin Luther King Fellows Press, 1986. Walker combines the theoretical and the practical on tithing to yield a useful model for financial stewardship. His writing is based on his actual experiences at his church.

Wimberly, Anne Steaty. *Soul Stories: African American Christian Education.* Nashville: Abingdon Press, 1994. Wimberly discusses the importance of education for the African American Christian. She provides a practical model for teaching adults and argues for the importance of understanding the unique needs of the African American community and its relationship to Christian education.

Wright, Jeremiah, Jr. "A Case Study in Black Church Renewal." In *Signs of the Kingdom in the Secular Society.* Edited by David Frenchak, et al. Chicago: Covenant Press, 1984.

Selected Resources on the African American Church

These books have been included and called "classic" because they were referred to by most of the authors listed above. In addition, scholars have recommended these works in the study of the African American church. It would be difficult, if not impossible, to truly understand the wisdom and uniqueness of the African American preacher without understanding the history of the African American church.

Du Bois, William E. B., ed. *The Negro Church.* Atlanta University, report no. 8, 1903. Atlanta: Atlanta University Publications, II, 1903. Reprint. New York: Arno Press and New York Times, 1969.

Frazier, E. Franklin. *The Negro Church in America.* New York: Shocken Press, 1974. Frazier discusses the religion of the slaves, the institutional church of the free Negroes, the "invisible institution," Negro religion in the city, and the black church and assimilation.

Harris, James H. *Pastoral Theology: A Black-Church Perspective*. Minneapolis: Augsburg Fortress Press, 1991. Harris offers a fresh view of the African American church and equates pastoral theology with liberation theology. The second part of the book gives practical advice on church administration, Christian education, worship, and preaching.

Lincoln, C. Eric. *The Black Experience in Religion: A Collection of Readings*. Garden City, N.Y.: Doubleday, 1974. A collection of essays on the black religious experience in the 1960s and 1970s. The book is divided into five chapters: "Black Religion and the Black Church"; "Black Preachers, Black Preaching, and Black Theology"; "Black Religion and Black Protest"; "Black Cults and Sects"; and "Black Religion in Africa and the Caribbean."

_____. *The Black Church Since Frazier*. New York: Schocken Press, 1974. In this book Lincoln discusses black theology and black power. He also discusses the influence of the Muslims in America and what their agenda is.

Lincoln, C. Eric, and Lawrence H. Mamiya. *The Black Church in the African American Experience*. Durham, N.C.: Duke University Press, 1990. A historical overview of seven mainline African American denominations. Based on interviews with over eighteen hundred African American clergy.

Mays, Benjamin E. *The Negro's God*. Boston: Chapman and Grimes, 1938.

Mays, Benjamin, and Joseph William Nicholson. *The Negro's Church*. New York: The Institute of Social and Religious Research, 1933. Discusses the origin of the church, the message of the minister, the church building and financing the black church, and the genius of the black church.

McCall, Emmanuel L. *Black Church Life-Styles*. Nashville: Broadman Press, 1986. McCall presents a series of essays by leading African American preachers such as Otis Moss and Ella Mitchell. Topics cover worship, preaching, hymnody, and outreach.

Raboteau, Albert J. *Slave Religion*. New York: Oxford University Press, 1978. An account of the religious life of the slaves. The author begins with a discussion of religious practices in the African diaspora. He then discusses the concepts of conversion, rebellion, and docility as they apply to the religious life in the slave community.

Sernett, Milton C. *Black Religion and American Evangelism.* Metuchen, N.J.: The Scarecrow Press, Inc., 1975. Contains sections on black preachers in the South, the gospel for the slaves, and evangelism in the South during slavery.

_____, ed. *Afro-American Religious History: A Documentary Witness.* Durham, N.C.: Duke University Press, 1985. A unique collection of fifty rare essays and documents that cover African American religious history from Africa to the present. Excerpts from the studies of Du Bois, Mays, and Frazier.

Taryor, Nya Kwiawon, Sr. *Impact of the African Tradition on African Christianity.* Chicago: Strugglers' Community Press, 1984. A historical survey of the planting of Christianity in Africa and the contributions of Africans to the growth, development, and spread of the faith.

Washington, Joseph R., Jr. *Black Religion: The Negro and Christianity in the United States.* Boston: Beacon Press, 1966. A controversial book in that it contended that the black church had no theology and was not authentically Christian. Washington argued that the black church should integrate with the white church so that it could experience true Christianity. Because of his stance, black theology was born.

Wilmore, Gayraud S. *Black Religion and Black Radicalism.* Maryknoll, N.Y.: Orbis Books, 1983. A historical-theological interpretation of the African American religious experience. Wilmore contends that black religion was deradicalized and black radicalism was dechristianized during the twentieth century. He proposes that there must be a reunion between black radicalism and black religion.

Woodson, Carter G. *The History of the Negro Church.* Washington, D.C.: The Associated Publishers, 1921. Discusses early missionaries, pioneer Negro preachers, the independent church movement through the Civil War, religious education for training, and the development of the African American church up until 1921.

Contributors

The following is included for each of this book's contributors:
1. Name and current position in ministry
2. Earned college degrees
3. Denominational affiliation:
   ABC/USA—American Baptist Churches in the U.S.A.
   AME—African Methodist Episcopal Church
   AMEZ—African Methodist Episcopal Zion Church
   CC/DOC—Christian Church/Disciples of Christ
   COG—Church of God
   COGAI—Church of God/Anderson, Indiana
   COGIC—Church of God in Christ
   EC—Episcopal Church
   ELCA—Evangelical Lutheran Churches of America
   ID—Interdenominational
   NBCA—National Baptist Convention of America
   NBC/USA—National Baptist Convention, U.S.A., Inc.
   ND—Nondenominational
   PNBC—Progressive National Baptist Convention
   PC—Presbyterian Church
   SBC—Southern Baptist Convention
   UCC—United Church of Christ
   UM—United Methodist Church
4. Preaching generation (A preaching generation is defined as any generation within the family where some member of the family

109

was a preacher. This includes any foreparents, aunts, uncles, cousins, and so on. In some instances, a generation was skipped; for instance, a contributor's grandparent may have been a preacher, but his or her father or mother was not.)

CONTRIBUTORS

Charles G. Adams
Pastor
Hartford Memorial Baptist
Church; Detroit, Mich.
B.A.—University of Michigan,
M.Div.—Harvard Divinity
School
ABC/USA, PNBC
Fourth Generation

John H. Adams
Senior Bishop
The African Methodist Episcopal
Church; Columbia, S.C.
A.B.—Johnson C. Smith College, S.T.D.—Boston University, Th.D.—Boston University
AME
Second Generation

T. Garrott Benjamin, Jr.
Pastor
Light of the World Christian
Church; Indianapolis, Ind.
B.S.—St. Louis University,
M.Div.—Christian Theological
Seminary, D.Min.—Christian
Theological Seminary
CC/DOC
First Generation

Cecil Bishop
Presiding Bishop
Third Episcopal District, African
Methodist Episcopal Zion Church;
Charlotte, North Carolina;
B.A.—Knoxville College,
M.Div.—Howard University

School of Divinity, S.T.M.—
Wesley Theological Seminary
AMEZ
First Generation

Ralph E. Blanks
Pastor
Zoar United Methodist Church,
Inc.; Philadelphia, Pa.
B.A.—Hendrix College,
M.Div.—Drew University
School of Theology
UM
First Generation

Charles E. Booth
Pastor
Mt. Olivet Baptist Church; Columbus, Ohio
B.A.—Howard University,
M.Div.—Eastern Baptist Theological Seminary, D.Min.—
United Theological Seminary
ABC/USA, PNBC
Fourth Generation

L. Venchael Booth
Pastor
Olivet Baptist Church; Cincinnati,
Ohio
B.A.—Alcorn State University,
M.Div.—Howard University
School of Divinity, M.A.—
University of Chicago
PNBC
Fourth Generation

Arthur Brazier
Pastor
Apostolic Church of God; Chicago, Ill.
B.A.—Moody Bible Institute
COG
Third Generation

Amos Brown
Pastor
Third Baptist Church; San Francisco, Calif.
B.A.—Morehouse College,
M.Div.—Crozer Theological Seminary, D.Min.—United Theological Seminary
ABC/USA, NBC/USA
Third Generation

Jesse Brown, Jr.
Pastor
Christ Lutheran Church; Philadelphia, Pa.
B.A.—Concordia College,
M.Div.—Lutheran School of Theology
ELCA
Second Generation

Cecelia Williams Bryant
Episcopal Supervisor
Tenth District of the A.M.E. Church; Houston, Tex.
AME
Fourth Generation

John R. Bryant
Bishop
Tenth District of the A.M.E. Church; Houston, Tex.
B.A.—Morgan University,
M.Th.—Boston University,
D.Min.—Colgate-Rochester Theological Seminary
AME
Second Generation

Calvin O. Butts III
Pastor
Abyssinian Baptist Church; New York, N.Y.
B.A.—Morehouse College,
M.Div.—Union Theological Seminary, D.Min.—Drew University
PNBC
First Generation

Albert Campbell
Pastor
Mt. Carmel Baptist Church; Philadelphia, Pa.
B.A.—Bishop College, M.Div.—Union Theological Seminary
ABC/USA, NBC/USA
Third Generation

Anthony Campbell
Pastor
Russell Street Baptist Church; Detroit, Mich.
B.A.—Howard University,
M.Div.—Boston University
NBC/USA
Second Generation

Katie G. Cannon
Professor
Temple University; Philadelphia, Pa.
B.S.—Barber-Scotia College,
M.Div.—Interdenominational Theological Center, Ph.D.—Union Theological Seminary
Presbyterian
First Generation

Delores Carpenter
Pastor
Michigan Park Christian Church; Washington, D.C.
B.A.—Morgan State University,
M.A.—Washington University,

M.Div.—Howard Divinity
School, Ed.D.—Rutgers Uni-
versity
CC/DOC
Third Generation

Lawrence E. Carter, Sr.
Dean
Martin Luther King, Jr., Interna-
tional Chapel; Morehouse Col-
lege; Atlanta, Ga.
B.A.—Virginia College,
M.Div.—Boston University
School of Theology, S.T.M.—
Boston University School of
Theology, Ph.D.—Boston Uni-
versity School of Theology
ABC/USA, NBC/USA, PNBC
Sixth Generation

Mack King Carter
Pastor
New Mt. Olive Baptist Church;
Ft. Lauderdale, Fla.
A.A.—Central Florida Commu-
nity College, B.A.—Univer-
sity of Florida,
M.Div.—Southern Baptist
Theological Seminary,
D.Min.—Southern Baptist
Theological Seminary
NBC/USA
First Generation

Caesar A. W. Clark
Pastor
Good Street Baptist Church; Dal-
las, Tex.
B.A.—Bishop College
NBC/USA
First Generation

Joy Clark
Pastor
St. Peter's Lutheran Church; New
York, N.Y.

B.A.—Queens College, M.A.—
New York University,
M.Div.—Union Theological
Seminary
ELCA
First Generation

Johnnie Colemon
Pastor
Christ Universal Temple; Chi-
cago, Ill.
B.A.—Wiley College
ND
First Generation

Suzan Johnson Cook
Pastor
Mariners' Temple Baptist
Church; New York, N.Y.
B.A.—Emerson College, M.A.—
Columbia Teachers College,
M.Div.—Union Theological
Seminary, D.Min.—United
Theological Seminary
ABC/USA
First Generation

J. Jerome Cooper
Pastor
Berean Presbyterian Church;
Philadelphia, Pa.
B.S.—Lincoln University,
M.Div.—Lincoln University
Seminary, D.Min.—Eastern
Baptist Theological Seminary
PC
First Generation

Evans E. Crawford
Professor, Social Ethics
Howard University School of Di-
vinity; Washington, D.C.
B.A.—Samuel Houston College,
STB—Boston University
School of Theology, Ph.D.—

Boston University Graduate School
UM
Second Generation

James H. Evans, Jr.
President
Colgate Rochester/Bexley Hall/Crozer Divinity School; Rochester, N.Y.
B.A.—University of Michigan, M.Div.—Yale Divinity School, Ph.D.—Union Theological Seminary
ABC/USA
Fourth Generation

Cain Hope Felder
Professor, New Testament Language and Literature
Howard University School of Divinity; Washington, D.C.
B.A.—Howard University, Diploma in Theology—Oxford University, Mansfield College, M.Div.—Union Theological Seminary, M.Ph.—Columbia University, Ph.D.—Columbia University/Union Theological Seminary
UM
First Generation

Robert M. Franklin
Director of Program, Black Church Studies
Emory University School of Religion; Atlanta, Ga.
B.A.—Morehouse College, M.Div.—Harvard Divinity School, Ph.D.—University of Chicago
COGIC
Fourth Generation

Catherine I. Godboldte
Author/Church Research Consultant
Philadelphia, Pa.
B.S.—St. Joseph's University, M.A.R.—Eastern Baptist Theological Seminary, Ph.D.—Temple University
ABC/USA,PNBC
Sixth Generation

Jacquelyn Grant
Professor of Systematic Theology
Interdenominational Theological Seminary; Atlanta, Ga.
B.A.—Bennett College, M.Div.—Interdenominational Theological Center, M.Ph.—Union Theological Seminary, Ph.D.—Union Theological Seminary
AME
Second Generation

William H. Gray III
Pastor
Bright Hope Baptist Church; Philadelphia, Pa.
B.A.—Franklin and Marshall College, M.Div.—Drew Theological Seminary, Th.M.—Princeton Theological Seminary
ABC/USA, NBC/USA, PNBC
Third Generation

Maurice Green
Pastor
Lily of the Valley COGIC; Bryan, Tex.
A.A.—Long Beach City College
COGIC
Second Generation

Arlee Griffin, Jr.
Pastor
Berean Missionary Baptist
Church; Brooklyn, N.Y.
B.A.—University of North Caro-
lina, M.Div.—Southeastern
Baptist Theological Seminary,
D.Min.—Boston University
ABC/USA, PNBC
First Generation

James Hall, Jr.
Pastor
Triumph Baptist Church; Phila-
delphia, Pa.
B.A.—Morris College, M.Div.—
Morris College Seminary
NBC/USA, PNBC
Third Generation

Forrest Harris
Assistant Dean/Director of the
Kelly Miller Smith Institute
Vanderbilt University; Nashville,
Tenn.
B.A.—Knoxville College,
B.Th.—American Baptist Col-
lege, M.Div.—Vanderbilt Uni-
versity, D.Min.—Vanderbilt
University
NBC/USA
Second Generation

James H. Harris
Pastor
Second Baptist Church; Rich-
mond, Va.
B.A.—Virginia State University,
M.Div.—Virginia Union
School of Theology, Ph.M.—
Old Dominion University,
D.Min.—United Theological
Seminary, Ph.D.—Old Domin-
ion University
ABC/USA, NBC/USA, PNBC
Second Generation

Michael N. Harris
Pastor
Wheat Street Baptist Church; At-
lanta, Ga.
B.A.—Morehouse College,
M.Div.—Eastern Baptist Theo-
logical Seminary, D.Min.—
Eastern Baptist Theological
Seminary
ABC/USA, PNBC
First Generation

Wallace S. Hartsfield
Pastor
Metropolitan Baptist Church;
Kansas City, Mo.
B.A.—Clark College, M.Div.—
Gammon Theological Semi-
nary/Interdenominational
Theological Center
NBCA
First Generation

William E. Hayman, Jr.
Pastor
Lutheran Church of the Living
Word; Columbia, Md.
B.S.—University of Delaware,
M.Div.—Lutheran Theological
Seminary at Philadelphia
ELCA
First Generation

Corneilius Henderson
President
Gammon Theological Seminary;
Atlanta, Ga.
B.A.—Clark College, M.Div.—
Gammon Theological Semi-
nary, S.T.M.—Gammon
Theological Seminary/Interde-
nominational Theological Cen-
ter
UM
First Generation

H. Beecher Hicks, Jr.
Pastor
Metropolitan Baptist Church;
Washington, D.C.
B.A.—University of Arkansas,
M.Div.—Colgate-Rochester
Theological Seminary,
D.Min.—Colgate-Rochester
Theological Seminary
PNBC
Third Generation

Sherman G. Hicks
Bishop
Metropolitan Chicago Synod;
Chicago, Ill.
B.A.—Wittenberg University,
M.Div.—Hamma School of
Theology
ELCA
First Generation

Zan Holmes
Pastor
Saint Luke Community United
Methodist Church; Dallas, Tex.
B.A.—Houston-Tillotson Col-
lege, B.D.—Perkins School of
Theology, M.T.S.—Perkins
School of Theology
UM
Second Generation

Alvin O. Jackson
Pastor
Mississippi Boulevard Christian
Church; Memphis, Tenn.
B.A.—Butler University,
M.Div.—Duke University
School of Divinity, D.Min.—
United Theological Seminary
CC/DOC
Second Generation

Jesse L. Jackson
President

The Rainbow Coalition; Washington, D.C.
B.A.—North Carolina Agricul-
tural and Technical State University
NBC/USA
First Generation

T. J. Jemison, Sr.
Pastor
Mt. Zion First Baptist Church;
Baton Rouge, La.
B.A.—Alabama State University,
M.Div.—Virginia Union Theo-
logical Seminary
NBC/USA
Third Generation

E. Edward Jones
Pastor
Galilee Baptist Church; Shreve-
port, La.
B.A.—Grambling State Univer-
sity, B.A.—Bishop College,
M.Div.—United Theological
Seminary (La.)
NBCA
Second Generation

G. Daniel Jones
Pastor
Grace Baptist Church of German-
town; Philadelphia, Pa.
B.S.—Virginia Union University,
M.Div.—Andover Newton
Theology School, D.Min.—
Howard University School of
Religion
ABC/USA
Third Generation

William A. Jones, Jr.
Pastor
Bethany Baptist Church; Brook-
lyn, N.Y.
B.A.—University of Kentucky,

M.Div.—Crozer Theological
Seminary, D.Min.—Colgate-
Rochester Theological Semi-
nary
PNBC
Third Generation

Thomas Kilgore, Jr.
Pastor Emeritus
Second Baptist Church; Los An-
geles, Calif.
B.A.—Morehouse College,
M.Div.—Union Theological
Seminary
ABC/USA, PNBC

Joseph E. Lowery
President
Southern Christian Leadership
Conference; Atlanta, Ga.
B.A.—Knoxville College, B.D.—
Wayne University, D.D.—
Payne Theological Seminary,
L.L.D.—Chicago Ecumenical
Institute
UM
Fourth Generation

Fred A. Lucas, Jr.
Pastor
Bridge Street African Methodist
Episcopal Church; Brooklyn,
N.Y.
B.A.—Harvard University,
M.Div.—Harvard Divinity
School, D.Min.—Colgate-
Rochester Theological Semi-
nary
AME
First Generation

J. Wendell Mapson, Jr.
Pastor
Monumental Baptist Church;
Philadelphia, Pa.
B.A.—Morehouse College,

M.Div.—Crozier Theological
Seminary, D.Min.—Eastern
Baptist Theological Seminary
NBC/USA
Second Generation

J. Wendell Mapson, Sr.
Pastor
Mt. Calvary Baptist Church;
Newark, N.J.
A.B.—Selma University, B.Th.—
Selma University
NBC/USA
First Generation

Floyd Massey, Jr.
Pastor Emeritus
Macedonia Baptist Church; Los
Angeles, Calif.
B.A.—Johnson C. Smith Col-
lege, M.Div.—Colgate-Roches-
ter Theological Seminary,
D.Min.—Colgate-Rochester
Theological Seminary
ABC/USA, NBC/USA
First Generation

James E. Massey
Academic Dean
Anderson University School of
Theology; Anderson, Ind.
B.A.—William Tyndale College,
M.A.R.—Oberlin Graduate
School of Theology, D.D.—As-
bury Theological Seminary
COGAI
Third Generation

Emmanuel McCall
Pastor
Christian Fellowship Baptist
Church; Atlanta, Ga.
B.A.—University of Louisville,
B.D.—Southern Baptist Theo-
logical Seminary, M.A.—
Southern Baptist Theological

Seminary, M.Div.—Southern
Baptist Theological Seminary,
D.Min.—Emory University
SB
First Generation

Vashti McKenzie
Pastor
Payne Memorial A.M.E. Church;
Baltimore, Md.
B.A.—University of Maryland,
M.Div.—Howard University
School of Divinity, D.Min.—
United Theological Seminary
AME
First Generation

Samuel B. McKinney
Pastor
Mt. Zion Baptist Church; Seattle,
Wash.
B.A.—Morehouse College,
M.Div.—Colgate-Rochester
Theological Seminary,
D.Min.—Colgate-Rochester
Theological Seminary
ABC/USA, NBC/USA
Third Generation

Ella P. Mitchell
Visiting Professor of Homiletics
Interdenominational Theological
Seminary; Atlanta, Ga.
B.A.—Taledega College,
M.Div.—Union Theological
Seminary, D.Min.—School of
Theology at Claremont
ABC/USA, NBC/USA
Second Generation

Frank B. Mitchell, Jr.
Pastor Emeritus
Pinn Memorial Baptist Church;
Philadelphia, Pa.
B.A.—Lincoln University
PNBC
Third Generation

Henry H. Mitchell
Visiting Professor of Homiletics
Interdenominational Theological
Center; Atlanta, Ga.
B.A.—Lincoln University,
B.D.—Union Theological
Seminary, M.A.—California
State University, Ph.D.—
School of Theology at Clare-
mont
ABC/USA, NBC/USA
Second Generation

William B. Moore
Pastor
Tenth Memorial Baptist Church;
Philadelphia, Pa.
B.A.—Fayetteville State,
M.Div.—Lutheran Theological
Seminary at Philadelphia
ABC/USA, NBC/USA
First Generation

Otis Moss, Jr.
Pastor
Olivet Baptist Church; Cleve-
land, Ohio
B.A.—Morehouse College,
M.Div.—Morehouse School of
Religion/Interdenominational
Theological Center, D.Min.—
United Theological Seminary
ABC/USA, PNBC
First Generation

Olin P. Moyd
Pastor
Mt. Lebanon Baptist Church; Bal-
timore, Md.
B.A.—Morgan State University,
M.Div.—Howard University
School of Divinity, Ph.D.—
Ecumenical Institute of Theology,
St. Mary's Seminary and Uni-
versity
ABC/USA, NBC/USA
Third Generation

Cecil Murray
Pastor
First African Methodist Episcopal Church; Los Angeles, Calif.
B.A.—Florida A & M University,
Rel.D.—School of Religion at
Claremont
AME
First Generation

Susan D. Newman
Pastor
First Congregational United
Church of Christ; Atlanta, Ga.
B.A.—George Washington University, M.Div.—Howard
School of Divinity, D.Min.—
United Theological Seminary
UCC
Fifth Generation

M. Marquette Peace, Jr.
Pastor
Zion Baptist Church; Brooklyn,
N.Y.
B.S.—Cheyney University,
M.A.R.—Eastern Baptist Theological Seminary
ABC/USA, PNBC
Second Generation

James C. Perkins
Pastor
Greater Christ Baptist Church;
Detroit, Mich.
B.A.—Wiley College, M.Div.—
Andover Newton Theological
School, D.Min.—United Theological Seminary
ABC/USA, PNBC
First Generation

Frederick K. C. Price
Pastor/Teacher
Crenshaw Christian Center; Los
Angeles, Calif.

Ph.D.—Friends International
Christian University
ND
First Generation

Samuel D. Proctor
Pastor Emeritus
Abyssinian Baptist Church; New
York, N.Y.
B.A.—Virginia Union University, M.Div.—Crozer Theological Seminary,
D.Min.—Colgate-Rochester
Theological Seminary
ABC/USA
Fourth Generation

Joe S. Ratliff
Pastor
Brentwood Baptist Church; Houston, Tex.
B.A.—Morehouse College,
M.Div.—Interdenominational
Theological Center, D.Min.—
Interdenominational Theological Center
SB
Third Generation

Frank M. Reid III
Pastor
Bethel African Methodist Episcopal Church; Baltimore, Md.
B.A.—Yale University, M.Div.—
Harvard Divinity School,
D.Min.—United Theological
Seminary
AME
Fifth Generation

J. Deotis Roberts
Distinguished Professor of Philosophical Thought
Eastern Baptist Theological Seminary; Philadelphia, Pa.
A.B.—Johnson C. Smith College,

B.D.—Shaw University,
S.T.M.—Hartford Theological
Seminary, Ph.D.—University
of Edinburgh, D.Litt.—University of Edinburgh
ABC/USA, PNBC
First Generation

Joseph L. Roberts, Jr.
Pastor
Ebenezer Baptist Church; Atlanta, Ga.
B.A.—Knoxville College,
M.Div.—Union Theological
Seminary, Th.M.—Princeton
Theological Seminary
ABC/USA, PNBC
Second Generation

Gus Roman
Pastor
Canaan Baptist Church; Philadelphia, Pa.
B.A.—Virginia Union University,
M.Div.—Howard University
ABC/USA, NBC/USA, PNBC
First Generation

Manuel L. Scott, Sr.
Pastor Emeritus
St. John Missionary Baptist
Church; Dallas, Tex.
B.A.—Bishop College
NBC/USA
First Generation

Beverly J. Shamana
Associate Council Director
United Methodist Center;
Pasadena, Calif.
B.A.—Occidental College,
M.Div.—Garrett-Evangelical
Theological Seminary
UM
First Generation

David T. Shannon, Sr.
President
Allen University; Columbia, S.C.
B.A.—Virginia Union University, B.D.—Virginia Union
University, S.T.M.—Oberlin
Graduate School of Theology,
D.Min.—Vanderbilt University, Ph.D.—University of
Pittsburgh
ABC/USA
First Generation

William J. Shaw
Pastor
White Rock Baptist Church;
Philadelphia, Pa.
B.A.—Bishop College, M.Div.—
Union Theological Seminary,
D.Min.—Colgate-Rochester
Theological Seminary
NBC/USA
First Generation

Marshall L. Shepard, Jr.
Pastor
Mt. Olivet Baptist Church; Philadelphia, Pa.
B.A.—Virginia Union University
PNBC
Fourth Generation

Benjamin Smith
Pastor
Deliverance Evangelistic Church;
Philadelphia, Pa.
Education done under private tutelage
ID
First Generation

Bennett W. Smith, Sr.
Pastor
St. John Baptist Church; Buffalo,
N.Y.

B.A.—Tennessee State University,
M.Div.—Colgate Rochester
ABC/USA, PNBC
First Generation

J. Alfred Smith, Sr.
Pastor
Allen Temple Baptist Church;
Oakland, Calif.
B.S.—Western Baptist College,
B.D.—Missouri School of Re-
ligion, Th.M.—Missouri
School of Religion, Th.M.—
American Baptist Seminary of
the West, D.Min.—Golden
Gate Seminary
ABC/USA, PNBC
First Generation

Mack H. Smith
Pastor
Trinity Lutheran Church; Wyan-
danch, N.Y.
B.A.—Roberts Wesleyan Col-
lege, M.Div.—Lutheran Theo-
logical Seminary at
Philadelphia
ELCA
First Generation

Nelson H. Smith, Jr.
Pastor
New Pilgrim Baptist Church; Bir-
mingham, Ala.
B.A.—Selma University
PNBC
Second Generation

Robert Johnson-Smith, Sr.
Pastor
Salem Baptist Church of Jenkintown
B.A.—Morehouse College,
M.Div.—Andover Newton
Theological Seminary,
S.T.M.—Andover Newton
Theological School, M.S.W.—

Bryn Mawr School of Social
Work, D.Min.—Andover New-
ton Theological School
ABC/USA, PNBC
Third Generation

Sara Potter Smith
President and Founder
Sara Potter Smith Community
Development Corporation;
Philadelphia, Pa.
B.A.—Temple University
UM
First Generation

Wallace C. Smith
Pastor
Shiloh Baptist Church; Washing-
ton, D.C.
B.A.—Villanova University,
M.Div.—Eastern Baptist Theo-
logical Seminary, D.Min.—
Eastern Baptist Theological
Seminary
ABC/USA, NBC/USA, PNBC
First Generation

Leon H. Sullivan
Pastor Emeritus
Zion Baptist Church; Philadel-
phia, Pa.
B.A.—West Virginia State Col-
lege, M.Div.—Union Theologi-
cal Seminary,
M.A.R.—Columbia University
NBC/USA
First Generation

Gardner C. Taylor
Pastor Emeritus
Concord Baptist Church of
Christ; Brooklyn, N.Y.
B.A.—Leland College, M.Div.—
Oberlin College
ABC/USA, PNBC
Second Generation

H. Dean Trulear
Dean
New York Theological Seminary;
New York, N.Y.
B.A.—Morehouse College,
Ph.D.—Drew University
ABC/USA, PNBC
First Generation

Wyatt Tee Walker
Pastor
Canaan Baptist Church; Harlem,
N.Y.
B.S.—Virginia Union, M.Div.—
Virginia Union School of Divinity,
D.Min.—Colgate-Rochester
Theological Seminary
NBC/USA, PNBC
Second Generation

Repsie Warren
Pastor
Society for Helping Church;
Philadelphia, Pa.
B.S.—Elizabeth City University,
Ed.M.—Antioch University,
M.A.R.—Lutheran Theological Seminary at Philadelphia,
D.Min.—New York Theological Seminary
ND
Second Generation

Paul Washington
Rector Emeritus
Church of the Advocate; Philadelphia, Pa.
A.B.—Lincoln University,
B.D.—Philadelphia Divinity School
EC
First Generation

William D. Watley
Pastor

St. James African Methodist Episcopal Church; Newark, N.J.
B.A.—St. Louis University,
M.Div.—Interdenominational Theological Center, Ph.D.—
Columbia University
AME
Second Generation

Renita J. Weems
Assistant Professor, Hebrew Bible
Vanderbilt University; Nashville,
Tenn.
B.A.—Wellesley College,
M.Ph.—Princeton Theological Seminary, Ph.D.—Princeton Theological Seminary
AME
First Generation

Dennis W. Wiley
Pastor
Covenant Baptist Church; Washington, D.C.
B.A.—Harvard University,
M.Div.—Howard University,
M.Ph.—Union Theological Seminary, Ph.D.—Union Theological Seminary
ABC/USA, PNBC, SBC
Third Generation

Cecil Williams
Pastor
Glide Memorial United Methodist Church; San Francisco,
Calif.
B.A.—Southern Methodist University
UM
First Generation

Jeremiah A. Wright, Jr.
Pastor
Trinity United Church of Christ;
Chicago, Ill.

B.A.—Howard University,
    M.A.—Howard University,
    M.A.—University of Chicago
    Divinity School, D.Min.—
    United Theological Seminary
UCC
Second Generation

Aidsand Wright-Riggins
Executive Minister
National Ministries, American
    Baptist Churches in the
    U.S.A.; Valley Forge, Pa.
B.A.—California State Univer-
    sity, M.Div.—American Bap-
    tist Seminary of the West
ABC/USA
First Generation

Prathia Hall Wynn
Pastor
Mt. Sharon Baptist Church; Phila-
    delphia, Pa.
B.A.—Temple University,
    M.Div.—Princeton Theologi-
    cal Seminary, M.S.T.—Prince-
    ton Theological Seminary
ABC/USA, PNBC
Second Generation

Johnny Ray Youngblood
Pastor
St. Paul Community Baptist
    Church; New York, N.Y.
B.A.—Dillard University,
    M.Div.—Colgate-Rochester
    Theological Seminary,
    D.Min.—United Theological
    Seminary
ABC/USA, PNBC
First Generation